The Persian Empire

*From Cyrus the Great to Alexander –
A Complete Overview of Ancient Persia*

By

Samuel Corwin

Table of Contents

Introduction
Why Persia Still Matters

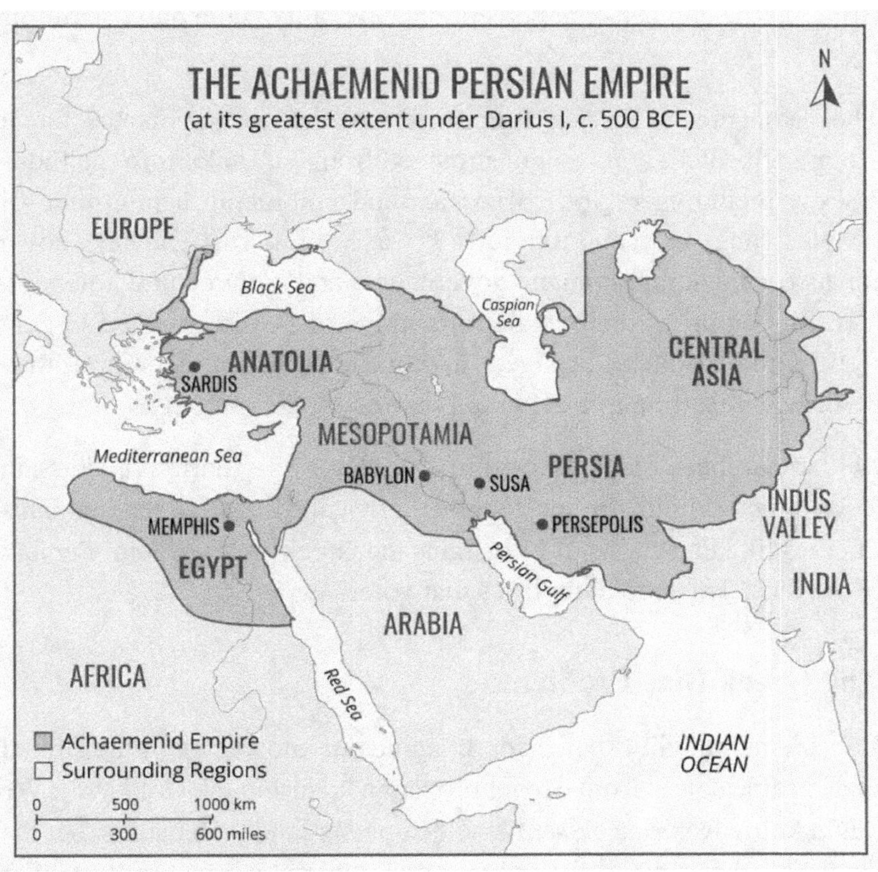

Persian Empire at Its Greatest Extent

For two and a half millennia, one of history's greatest empires has been viewed primarily through the lens of its adversaries.

When people think of ancient Persia, they often visualize Xerxes - the imposing, gold-adorned ruler from *300*, launching vast armies against a few valiant Greeks. It's a narrative filled with despotism, excess, and eventual defeat. However, this perception obscures a crucial truth: the Persian Empire was one of the most advanced, tolerant, and administratively sophisticated civilizations of the ancient world. Bridging the gap between perception and reality is the purpose of this book.

The Achaemenid Persian Empire, established by Cyrus the Great around 550 BCE, at its height stretched from the Balkans to the Indus Valley, including regions of Africa and embracing a multitude of peoples, languages, and religions. It was not just vast but was known for its organization, humane governance, and architectural splendor. Yet, for centuries, the prevalent narrative of Persia emerged largely from Greek writers engaged in conflicts with the empire they described, resulting in a depiction marred by bias and distortion.

Modern archaeology has begun to reshape this narrative. Persian inscriptions, administrative documents, royal edicts, and the remnants of cities like Persepolis offer insights the Greeks never could: Persia's own voice. This book amplifies that voice.

The Greek Bias Problem

Consider a thought experiment. Imagine our knowledge of the United States came solely from Soviet propaganda during the Cold War. We might know America existed, wielded power, and won battles, but the depth of American life, values, and beliefs would be lost. For centuries, this was similar to how historians understood ancient Persia.

Greek historians like Herodotus and Thucydides were insightful observers, but Persia was their rival - a contrast to Greek "freedom" versus Persian "tyranny," serving specific political purposes rather than objective description.

Herodotus, often dubbed the Father of History, wrote significantly about Persia, displaying occasional empathy. Yet, he wrote as an outsider, for a Greek audience, with innate Greek biases. His depiction of the Persian Wars in the early fifth century BCE molded Western perceptions of Persia for millennia.

Following writers painted less favorable pictures. By the time Alexander the Great conquered the Achaemenid Empire in 330 BCE, the narrative of decadence and inevitable decline was entrenched. Alexander's historians had every reason to depict the empire as corrupt, justifying its conquest. Although these histories endured, Persian perspectives largely vanished.

What Archaeology Changes

Archaeological finds beneath Persepolis - such as clay tablets inscribed in Elamite, the Persian administrative language - reveal the mundane yet revolutionary: payroll records. Workers who constructed Darius I's palaces received rations of wine, grain, and silver. Women were remunerated equally in certain roles, skilled laborers earned more, and additional rations were provided for pregnant workers and new mothers.

This narrative didn't align with Greek portrayals of Persian despotism and thus doesn't appear in their accounts. These Persepolis Fortification Tablets are just one example of how physical evidence has altered our understanding of the empire. Royal inscriptions, road networks, and artifacts from across its expanse reveal an empire thoughtfully governed, balancing central authority with local flexibility.

Cyrus the Great left behind the Cyrus Cylinder, discovered in Babylon in 1879. This document records policies allowing conquered peoples to return to their homelands and maintain their religions. Whether this reflects genuine tolerance or political calculation - or both - remains debated, but it highlights that Persian imperialism wasn't solely about domination.

Darius I expanded the empire and left detailed inscriptions like those at Behistun, which explain his conquests and vision of order. These proclamations, though propagandistic, were created from a Persian viewpoint, offering insights into their worldview.

How This Book Is Different

Many popular histories of ancient Persia rely heavily on Greek sources, supplementing them with archaeology when convenient. This book reverses that approach.

Persian sources take precedence, with Greek accounts used selectively and critically, acknowledging their agendas and limitations. Where Greek and Persian sources conflict, both are examined, and conclusions are drawn from the evidence rather than assuming Greek accuracy.

Honesty about uncertainties is crucial. The ancient world provides few certainties, with approximations and contested interpretations. Acknowledging ambiguity is essential. This book aims not to replace one myth with another but to portray the empire as it was: complex, contradictory, and extraordinary.

Key Takeaways

- The Persian Achaemenid Empire, founded around 550 BCE, was one of the most expansive and sophisticated ancient civilizations, from the Balkans to the Indus Valley.

- Greek sources, written by rivals or enemies, shaped Western perceptions of Persia with bias and distortion.

- Archaeological discoveries, like the Persepolis Fortification Tablets and Behistun relief, provide authentic Persian insights that challenge Greek narratives.

- Cyrus the Great founded the empire by uniting Iranian tribes and conquering neighbors; Darius I expanded it with systematic governance.

- The Cyrus Cylinder records Persian policies of religious and cultural tolerance, distinguishing the Achaemenid Empire from many contemporaries.

- This book prioritizes Persian and archaeological sources, treats Greek accounts critically, and clearly distinguishes between established facts and interpretations.

- Accurately understanding Persia is vital both for correcting historical records and for recognizing the empire's innovations that influenced subsequent empires.

What Cyrus constructed in the sixth century BCE was not merely a state; it was a blueprint. The administrative frameworks, road systems, cultural tolerance, and the use of satraps to govern distant territories would resonate through Alexander's realm, the Roman Empire, and beyond. To comprehend ancient power structures, you must first understand Persia - and to understand Persia, you must be willing to challenge centuries of misrepresentation.

Thus, we begin our journey.

PART 1
BEFORE EMPIRE

Chapter 1
The World Before Cyrus

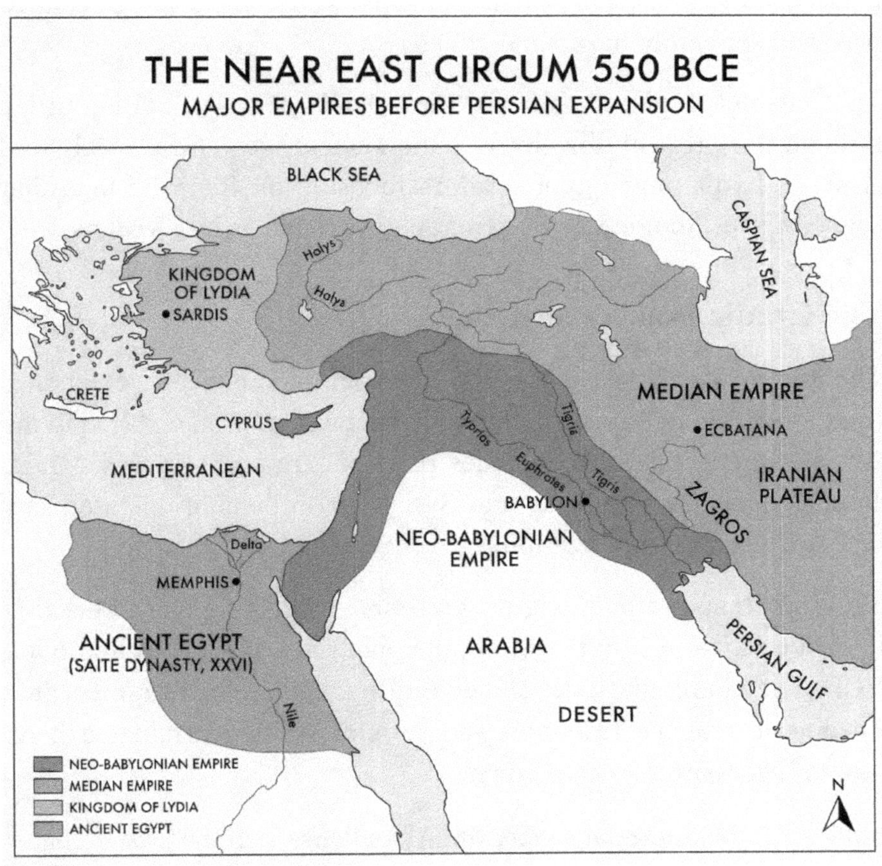

Major Powers Before Persian Expansion

Long before Cyrus the Great emerged from the Iranian plateau to leave his mark on the ancient world, the Near East had already witnessed the rise and fall of great civilizations. Empires had expanded their realms and complex societies flourished, driven by human ingenuity and conflict.

To appreciate Cyrus - his lasting achievements and enduring significance - one must first understand the world he inherited. It was not a simple array of kingdoms, but a dynamic and tumultuous landscape of competing powers and deep-seated histories. The stage was well set before his arrival.

This chapter explores this historical landscape. We will journey through the great civilizations of the ancient Near East - Babylon, Assyria, Lydia, and Egypt - before focusing on Iran, the land that shaped Cyrus, molded by its geography as much as by its rulers.

The Cradle Was Never Quiet

The ancient Near East is a complex geographic concept, extending from modern-day Egypt and Turkey in the west to Iran and Iraq in the east - a region that now includes parts of Armenia, Cyprus, Israel, Jordan, Lebanon, Palestine, and Syria. For millennia, this area saw repeated waves of civilization.

The Sumerians were among the earliest, establishing one of the first known civilizations in the Mesopotamian river valleys around 6500 BCE. They built cities, developed writing, and created sophisticated systems to manage resources and people. Writing originated here, born of necessity for accounting.

Following the Sumerians were the Akkadians, then the Babylonians, who made landmark contributions: codifying laws under Hammurabi and making astronomical observations that influenced later civilizations. The Hittites brought innovation in warfare with their chariot techniques and metalwork.

Each civilization contributed not only physical remnants but also ideas and technologies that later powers would adopt and adapt.

This cycle of conquest, absorption, and transmission defined the ancient Near East. While empires rose and fell, human knowledge continued to accumulate.

Assyria: Empire by Terror

Of all the powers before Cyrus, none cast a longer shadow than Assyria. From approximately 912 to 612 BCE, the Neo-Assyrian Empire was an unparalleled military force. Its armies were disciplined, its siege technologies advanced, and its rulers calculated in their ruthless strategies.

Assyrian kings systematically deported conquered peoples, relocating entire populations to disrupt local identities and weaken resistance. This policy of cultural dismemberment also claimed an unexpected benefit: it facilitated the spread of languages, crafts, religions, and knowledge. Displaced artisans and scholars disseminated their skills across the empire, fueling cultural diffusion.

By 612 BCE, the Assyrian Empire had collapsed, overthrown by a coalition including the Babylonians and the Medes, an Iranian people soon central to Cyrus's story. Although Assyria's physical presence faded, its legacy of interconnected, multicultural exchange endured.

Babylon: Law, Stars, and Ambition

Following Assyria's collapse, Babylon emerged as the dominant power under the Neo-Babylonian kings, particularly Nebuchadnezzar II. Babylon was celebrated for its achievements: legendary hanging gardens, pioneering astronomical records, and sophisticated legal traditions stemming back to Hammurabi.

By the time of Cyrus, Babylon carried immense symbolic weight. To conquer Babylon was a profound statement of power, and every empire-builder recognized its importance as a prize of geopolitical and cultural legitimacy.

Lydia: Wealth at the Edge of the World

To the west, Lydia flourished in what is now Turkey, renowned for its wealth and credited with minting the world's first true coinage. Its last king, Croesus, became synonymous with prosperity.

Lydia bordered the Greek world to the west and the emerging Persian power to the east. It was a prosperous buffer state, confident in its affluence and alliances - until Cyrus made it one of his early conquests, a tale explored in later chapters.

Egypt: Ancient Beyond Memory

Egypt stood apart in the Near East, distinct in geography and culture. Guarded by deserts and sustained by the Nile, Egypt developed a civilization notable for its continuity. By Cyrus's birth, Egypt was an entity of formidable age and identity.

Egypt's relationship with the broader Near East involved trade, conflict, and cultural exchange, yet it maintained a strong sense of identity rooted in its natural rhythms and divine monarchy. This resilience persisted even under foreign domination, presenting challenges to later Persian rulers.

Iran: The Land That Made the People

No civilization existed in isolation; geography influenced history. This was particularly true for Iran.

The Iranian plateau is a harsh environment, dominated by mountains and deserts. The Zagros Mountains, the Alborz range, and the Kopet Dag form natural barriers, while interior deserts like the Dasht-e Kavir and Dasht-e Lut offer scant hospitality. Iran demanded strategic resilience.

The mountain passes through the Zagros connected the plateau to Mesopotamia, controlling the movement of armies, goods, and ideas. Iran thus held a crucial strategic position in the ancient world.

The challenging environment fostered mobile, adaptable communities. Nomadism thrived in the highlands, and ingenious irrigation methods sustained agriculture. The Iranian peoples were not passive - they were proactive.

Iran also provided a defensible depth absent in river valley civilizations. Invaders faced a daunting terrain where local knowledge was paramount. Iran was difficult to conquer and impossible to overlook.

By the time the Medes, an Iranian people, helped overthrow the Assyrian Empire in 612 BCE, the plateau had produced organized, capable societies for centuries. Cyrus would be the epitome of this tradition.

Key Takeaways

- The ancient Near East, spanning from Egypt and Turkey to Iran and Iraq, was home to successive civilizations over millennia.

- Sumerians initiated writing and urban systems; Babylonians advanced legal and astronomical traditions; Hittites innovated in warfare.

- The Neo-Assyrian Empire (912-612 BCE) wielded unmatched military power and cultural diffusion through forced migrations.

- Babylon, after Assyria's fall, became a center of learning and a symbol of legitimacy sought by conquerors.

- Lydia, in Anatolia, introduced early coinage and straddled Greek and Persian influences.

- Egypt's isolation and cultural depth made it a resilient and unique Near Eastern power, challenging even for conquerors.

- Iran's geography created a strategically vital yet defensible region, shaping adaptable peoples capable of exerting power.

What the ancient Near East had built over millennia was more than kingdoms; it was a complex world, interconnected and primed for change. The empires that Cyrus would challenge were established and proud, each with its traditions of authority and governance. None foresaw that the transformative force would arise from the eastern plateau, led by a man skilled not only at conquest but at reigning.

Chapter 2
The Rise of the Persians and Medes

Before Cyrus the Great reshaped the ancient world, there were the Medes - a people whose kingdom, forged from ambition and the mountains, became intertwined with the empire that eventually eclipsed them.

Few historical narratives unfold with the speed and impact of the rise of the Iranian peoples during the first millennium BC. Over roughly four centuries, two interlinked groups - the Medes and the Persians - transformed from scattered tribes into the architects of the largest empire the world had yet seen. Understanding this transformation requires examining their beginnings in the rugged mountain terrains.

Newcomers in the Zagros

Around 1000 BC, the Medes began to settle along the northern Zagros Mountains, a formidable spine extending through present-day northwestern Iran. They were part of a larger migration of Western Iranian peoples - linguistically and ethnically akin groups establishing themselves across the highlands.

Life in the Zagros was harsh. The terrain was unforgiving, winters severe, and the political environment perilous. The Neo-Assyrian Empire, a dominant and militarized power, loomed over the region, extracting tribute and imposing its rule with ruthless efficiency.

For much of the 10th to 7th centuries BC, the Medes lived under Assyria's shadow, paying tribute and enduring raids. Yet, over time, their survival evolved into something greater.

The Median Kingdom: Order from the Mountains

By around 750 BC, the Medes were no longer merely tribal groups clinging to the highlands; they had begun to form a coherent political entity. The Median Kingdom, with its capital at Ecbatana (modern-day Hamadan in Iran), emerged as a regional power.

Ecbatana, situated at high elevation, was naturally defensible and strategically positioned as a hub between the Iranian plateau and the fertile lowlands. Ancient accounts describe it as grand, though details are sparse. Ecbatana provided a center around which political authority could crystallize.

The consolidation of the Median Kingdom was driven by the need for survival in the face of Assyrian threats, encouraging smaller groups to unite. Additionally, leadership structures developed to organize larger populations for warfare and administration. The Medes were learning statecraft.

The Fall of Assyria and the Median Moment

Despite its power, the Neo-Assyrian Empire was not invulnerable. By the late 7th century BC, internal strife, overexpansion, and rising rivals weakened its foundations.

In 612 BC, these weaknesses culminated in a dramatic collapse. A coalition including the Medes, Babylonians, Scythians, and Cimmerians struck decisive blows against Assyria. Nineveh, the great capital, fell, and the empire crumbled.

For the Medes, this was a defining achievement. With Assyria vanquished, they emerged as a principal power, controlling extensive territories. However, this new balance of power was unstable, with strong players occupying the region: Babylon to the south, Lydia to the west, Egypt, and the Medes. This fragile equilibrium lasted a generation before the rise of the Persians.

The Early Persians and the Achaemenid Line

While the Medes consolidated their kingdom, another Iranian group - the Persians - established themselves in the south, in what would become known as Persia or Pars (modern Fars province).

The Persians, ethnically and culturally related to the Medes, developed a different trajectory under the Achaemenid dynasty. The origins of this dynasty trace back to a figure named Achaemenes, though details remain elusive. By the 7th century BC, Persian rulers began consolidating power in Anshan and Pars, initially within the Median sphere of influence, as junior partners.

This arrangement would soon shift.

Cyrus and the Reversal of Fortune

In 550 BC, a Persian king named Cyrus - later known as "the Great" - seized a transformative moment by conquering the Median Kingdom.

This conquest was more than a military victory; it represented a radical political shift in the Near East. Cyrus, as the Achaemenid ruler, overthrew the Median king and integrated the Median state into a new, expansive Persian Empire. Ecbatana became a royal city in this empire, symbolizing that Cyrus was not merely erasing the past but building upon it.

Cyrus's success stemmed from his extraordinary leadership - tactically astute, politically shrewd, and capable of rallying diverse peoples. He also inherited the sophisticated structures established by the Medes. Their administrative systems, military traditions, and networks transitioned intact into Persian hands. In essence, the Medes laid the groundwork for the empire that followed.

A Pivotal Transition

The emergence of the Medes and Persians marked a pivotal shift in the scale of political organization in the ancient Near East. Previously dominated by smaller kingdoms and city-states, the region now witnessed the rise of an empire stretching from the Aegean to India, governed by a single dynasty with a unified vision.

This story, which unfolds further in subsequent chapters, finds its roots in the mountain settlements of the Zagros, the coalition that felled Nineveh, and the strategic power consolidation of the Persian dynasty.

Quick Summary

- Around 1000 BC, the Medes settled in the northern Zagros Mountains as part of a broader Iranian migration.

- From the 10th to 7th centuries BC, they endured Assyrian dominance, paying tribute and surviving incursions.

- By 750 BC, the Medes had formed a cohesive kingdom centered on Ecbatana.

- In 612 BC, a coalition including the Medes toppled the Neo-Assyrian Empire, elevating the Medes to a significant regional power.

- The Persians, related to the Medes, developed in Pars under the Achaemenid dynasty, initially within the Median influence.

- In 550 BC, Cyrus the Great of Persia conquered the Median Kingdom, founding the Achaemenid Empire and incorporating Median institutions.

- The Medes provided the administrative and political foundations for the Persian Empire.

The story of the Medes is one of integration - rising, dominating, and then being absorbed into a larger entity. However, they were not erased. When Cyrus established his empire, he built it on Median achievements, and that world endured for two centuries.

PART 2
THE BIRTH OF EMPIRE

Chapter 3
Cyrus the Great

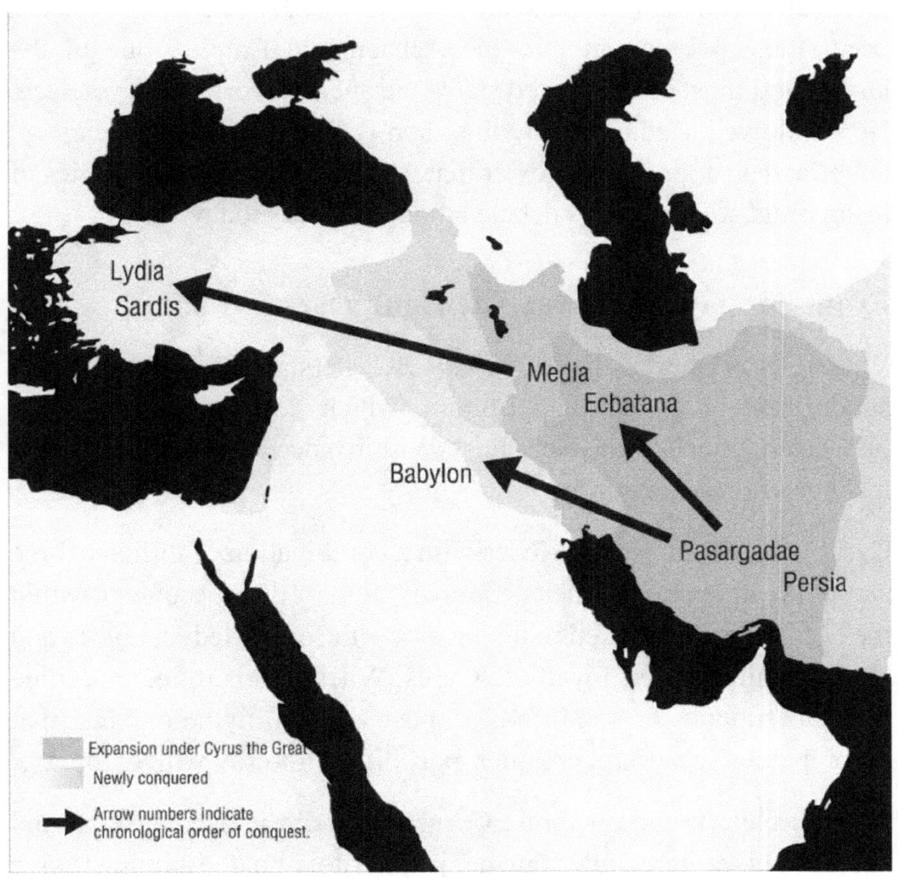

Expansion Under Cyrus the Great

A king who conquered half the known world and then told his new subjects they were free - that was Cyrus the Great. Not free from his rule, exactly, but free to worship their gods, speak their languages, and return to the homelands from which earlier conquerors had torn them. In an age when victory typically meant enslavement, plunder, and the erasure of the defeated's culture, Cyrus did something genuinely unusual. He won, and then he chose restraint.

That choice - repeated across three of the ancient world's most consequential conquests - made Cyrus not just a military force but a political phenomenon. Between 559 and 530 BC, he transformed a small Persian kingdom into the Achaemenid Empire, one of the largest and most sophisticated states the ancient world had ever seen. He swallowed Media, then Lydia, then Babylon itself. At each step, he refined an approach to power that would echo through centuries of history and still provokes debate among scholars today.

From Persia to Empire: The Conquest of Media

When Cyrus came to power in 559 BC, Persia was a vassal state - subordinate to the Median Empire, which dominated the Iranian plateau and much of the Near East. Within a decade, that relationship had been reversed entirely.

Cyrus moved against the Medes with a combination of military force and political cunning. Ancient sources suggest that discontent within the Median ranks worked in his favor - with some Median nobles and soldiers shifting their loyalty to Cyrus. Whether this reflects genuine popular support or the kind of post-victory mythologizing that accompanies successful conquerors is difficult to say with certainty.

What is clear is the outcome: Cyrus defeated the Median king and absorbed his empire, inheriting not just territory but the administrative infrastructure and prestige that came with it.

This was the foundation. Media provided Cyrus the resources and reach to look westward - toward a kingdom famous above all else for the wealth of its king.

The Fall of Croesus and the Riches of Lydia

Croesus of Lydia was, by ancient reputation, the richest man alive. His kingdom, centered in what is now western Turkey, sat at the crossroads of Greek and Near Eastern trade. Lydia produced some of the world's earliest coinage, and Croesus had accumulated wealth on a scale that turned his name into a byword for fortune.

He was also, by most accounts, badly misinformed about Cyrus.

According to the Greek historian Herodotus, Croesus consulted the Oracle at Delphi before marching against the Persians and received the famous prophecy that if he crossed the Halys River, he would destroy a great empire. He crossed. He was right about the empire - it was his own. Cyrus defeated him, and Lydia fell into Persian hands.

The conquest of Lydia was more than a military victory. It brought the Achaemenid Empire into direct contact with the Greek world for the first time, absorbing the Greek cities of the Ionian coast along with Lydia's legendary treasury. Croesus's wealth flowed into Persian coffers, amplifying the empire's capacity for further expansion. Cyrus had now stretched his reach from the Iranian plateau to the Aegean Sea.

But the greatest prize still lay to the south.

Babylon: The Jewel of the Ancient World

No city in the ancient Near East carried more symbolic weight than Babylon. It was the seat of civilization, the home of Marduk - the supreme god of the Babylonian pantheon - and the capital of an empire that had dominated Mesopotamia for generations. To take Babylon was to claim, in the eyes of the ancient world, something close to universal kingship. In 539 BC, Cyrus took it.

His opponent was Nabonidus, the last native king of Babylon, whose reign had been troubled by religious controversy. Nabonidus had elevated the moon god Sin above Marduk, alienating the powerful Babylonian priesthood and, according to some accounts, neglecting the traditional rituals that bound the king to the city's divine order.

Whether this religious rift genuinely weakened Babylonian resistance or whether later Persian accounts exaggerated it to justify the conquest, the result was the same: Cyrus entered Babylon, and Nabonidus was captured.

Ancient sources, including the Babylonian Chronicle, describe the fall of the city as relatively peaceful - a striking contrast to the brutal sieges and sackings that punctuated so much ancient warfare. Cyrus presented himself not as a foreign conqueror but as the rightful king chosen by Marduk himself to restore proper order to the city. He participated in Babylonian religious ceremonies, refrained from looting the temples, and chose not to deport the population.

This was a deliberate performance of legitimacy, and it worked.

The Cyrus Cylinder: A Document Unlike Any Other

Among the objects recovered from the ruins of ancient Babylon, one small clay cylinder stands apart. Roughly the size of a human fist, inscribed in cuneiform script, the Cyrus Cylinder is the most direct surviving record of how Cyrus chose to present his rule to the world - or at least to the world of Babylon.

Created as a foundation deposit following the conquest of 539 BC, the cylinder was buried in the walls of the city, as was customary for royal inscriptions. It was not meant for public display. It was a message to the gods, a declaration embedded in the very structure of the city Cyrus now claimed to govern.

What it says is remarkable. Cyrus presents himself as the chosen servant of Marduk, sent to liberate Babylon from Nabonidus's misrule. He describes restoring the city's sanctuaries, returning divine statues that had been displaced, and allowing peoples who had been deported under previous rulers to return to their homelands. He frames conquest not as domination but as restoration - a king giving back what had been wrongfully taken.

Historians debate how much of this reflects genuine policy and how much is royal propaganda crafted to pacify a newly conquered population. The answer is likely both. Cyrus had real strategic reasons to maintain stability in Babylon - a restive, resentful population would have been costly to control. But the ideology expressed in the cylinder also appears consistent with how Cyrus governed: a preference for accommodation over suppression, for co-opting local elites rather than replacing them.

The Jewish Exile and the Biblical Cyrus

One of the most striking consequences of the Babylonian conquest was its effect on a people far from the center of power. The Jews had been deported to Babylon by Nebuchadnezzar decades earlier, their Temple in Jerusalem destroyed, their community scattered. Cyrus, according to both the Cyrus Cylinder and the Hebrew Bible, reversed this. He permitted the Jewish exiles to return to their homeland and supported the rebuilding of the Temple in Jerusalem.

In the Book of Ezra, Cyrus issues a decree authorizing this return. In the Book of Isaiah, he is called the Lord's "anointed" - the only non-Jewish figure in the Hebrew Bible to receive that title. For the Jewish people, Cyrus was not a foreign king to be tolerated; he was an instrument of divine will.

This is a remarkable thing. A Persian conqueror, celebrated in the sacred texts of a people he had never directly conquered, honored across millennia for an act of political generosity that cost him relatively little but meant everything to those who received it. Whether Cyrus acted from genuine humanitarian impulse, shrewd political calculation, or some combination of the two, the effect was the same: real people returned to their homes. A community survived.

An Enlightened Conqueror - or a Skilled Politician?

Later writers, particularly the Greek historian Xenophon, portrayed Cyrus as something close to the ideal ruler - wise, just, merciful, and beloved by those he conquered. Xenophon's *Cyropaedia*, a semi-fictional biography of the Persian king, became one of the most widely read texts in the ancient world and shaped how later leaders - including Julius Caesar and Thomas Jefferson - thought about power and governance.

That portrait is almost certainly idealized. Cyrus was a conqueror, and conquest is never clean. His campaigns involved real violence, real displacement, and real coercion. The tolerance and accommodation he extended to Babylonians and Jews was not a universal policy applied to all peoples equally - it was a calculated approach to managing a diverse and far-flung empire.

But the calculation itself matters. In a world where the default response to conquest was terror and suppression, Cyrus consistently chose a different model. He recognized that an empire held together by fear alone is brittle, that local loyalty - bought through respect for local customs and gods - is more durable than loyalty extracted by force. That insight, expressed in clay and cuneiform on a small cylinder buried in a Babylonian wall, proved to be one of the most consequential ideas in the history of governance.

Key Takeaways

- Cyrus the Great reigned from 559 to 530 BC and founded the Achaemenid Empire through the successive conquests of Media, Lydia, and Babylon.

- His defeat of Croesus of Lydia brought enormous wealth into Persian hands and extended the empire's reach to the Aegean coast.

- Babylon fell to Cyrus in 539 BC; the city's last native king, Nabonidus, had alienated the powerful Babylonian priesthood, which may have eased the Persian takeover.

- Cyrus presented himself as a liberator and restorer rather than a conqueror - participating in Babylonian religious rites and claiming to act on behalf of the god Marduk.

- The Cyrus Cylinder, a cuneiform inscription buried as a foundation deposit in Babylon, records his policies of religious tolerance and the return of displaced peoples to their homelands.

- Cyrus permitted Jewish exiles to return to Judah and supported the rebuilding of the Temple in Jerusalem - an act celebrated in the Hebrew Bible, where he is called the Lord's anointed.

- Later writers, including Xenophon, idealized Cyrus as a model ruler; while that portrait is romanticized, his approach to governance - accommodation over suppression - was genuinely distinctive for his era.

Cyrus died in 530 BC, still campaigning on the empire's eastern frontier. He left behind a state that stretched from the Aegean to the edges of Central Asia, held together not by brute force alone but by a governing philosophy that treated diversity as something to be managed rather than eliminated. That philosophy would be tested, refined, and sometimes abandoned by the rulers who followed him -

but it never entirely disappeared. The small clay cylinder buried in the ruins of Babylon outlasted the empire it celebrated by more than two millennia, and the questions it raises about power, tolerance, and the obligations of the conqueror remain as alive today as they were in 539 BC.

Chapter 4

Cambyses and Egypt

Cyrus the Great built an empire. His son Cambyses II set out to expand it - aiming for the banks of the Nile.

Upon inheriting the Persian throne in 529 BCE, Cambyses governed the largest empire the ancient world had yet seen. Persia stretched from the Aegean coast to Central Asia's borders, but one prize remained: Egypt, ancient and wealthy, a civilization enduring for millennia before Persia's rise. Cambyses spent his reign pursuing this prize, with his conquest revealing both the ambitions and fault lines of the Achaemenid Empire.

His reign, lasting only seven years from 529 to 522 BCE, reshaped the ancient world.

A Kingdom Inherited, A Campaign Planned

Cambyses approached the Egyptian campaign neither unprepared nor impulsively. The conquest was foreseen even before he ascended the throne. Cyrus II had laid the groundwork, and the campaign Cambyses launched in 525 BCE fulfilled his father's strategic vision rather than sheer personal ambition.

Before becoming king, Cambyses held significant authority. By 538 BCE, he bore the title "king of Babylon" while Cyrus held "king of the lands" - a deliberate setup to give Cambyses experience in governance. This was no accident. Cyrus was grooming his successor for the burden of empire.

Upon Cyrus's death in 529 BCE, Cambyses inherited more than a throne; he inherited an ongoing project.

The Egyptian Campaign

The conquest of Egypt in 525 BCE stands as one of the ancient world's most significant military operations. Cambyses led his forces across the Sinai into Egypt, confronting Pharaoh Psamtik III, a ruler newly in power and yet to consolidate his position.

Psamtik III was defeated. While battle details are scant, the outcome was decisive: Egypt fell, and Cambyses became pharaoh, adding the ancient kingdom to the Achaemenid Empire's impressive domains.

What followed is where the historical record turns complex.

Herodotus, writing over a century later, depicted Cambyses as erratic and cruel - a king who desecrated temples, mocked religious customs, and acted with conqueror's contempt rather than ruler's wisdom. He described Cambyses stabbing the sacred Apis bull in mockery, portraying a king on the brink of madness.

Other evidence, however, complicates this portrayal. Some Egyptian sources suggest Cambyses initially adopted a more conciliatory approach, presenting himself as a legitimate pharaoh, respecting certain traditions, and integrating Egypt through accommodation rather than domination. This mirrored the model Cyrus used in Babylon: conquer the body, but honor the spirit.

Historians differ on reconciling these accounts. What seems clear is that Cambyses' relationship with Egypt was neither as catastrophic as Herodotus claimed nor as seamless as his defenders argue. The truth likely lies in between.

The Shadow of Bardiya

While Cambyses was in Egypt, a crisis was brewing at home, possibly due to a decision made before his campaign.

According to the Behistun Inscription, a monumental text by later king Darius I, Cambyses secretly killed his brother Bardiya - known to the Greeks as Smerdis - to eliminate a potential rival. However, the inscription, a politically motivated document, was created by one with every reason to justify his own power grab, so it must be read with caution.

What is undisputed is what followed. In March 522 BCE, a man claiming to be Bardiya rebelled against Cambyses' rule, gathering notable support, suggesting widespread discontent with Cambyses' reign. Economic hardship might have contributed, as evidence points to famine conditions in Babylonia during this period, a tenuous foundation for maintaining imperial control.

The Limits of Empire

Cambyses never returned to quell the rebellion. He died in July 522 BCE under unclear circumstances, whether by accident, illness, or more nefarious means. His death abruptly ended a reign that achieved remarkable feats - like the absorption of Egypt into the Persian Empire - while exposing the empire's fragility during a ruler's absence and political turbulence.

Darius I, who eventually suppressed the Bardiya rebellion and seized the throne, was engaged in the imperial administration during Cambyses' Egyptian campaign. His proximity to power amidst the 522 BCE chaos has led some historians to view it as not merely a succession crisis but as an opportunity seized by someone who understood that instability could bring opportunity.

The limits of Achaemenid expansion were not merely geographic. They were logistical, political, and human. The empire, extending from Egypt to Central Asia, needed more than military might for cohesion. It required diligent administrative oversight, economic management, and loyal cultivation across diverse peoples and traditions. Cambyses demonstrated that Persia could conquer Egypt, but the challenge remained in ruling it - and in maintaining the empire's stability.

30

Key Takeaways

- Cambyses II ruled Persia from 529 to 522 BCE, inheriting the empire Cyrus the Great built.

- The 525 BCE conquest of Egypt was planned under Cyrus and executed by Cambyses against Pharaoh Psamtik III.

- Herodotus depicts Cambyses as tyrannical and erratic, but other sources suggest a more nuanced governance of Egypt.

- Cambyses allegedly killed his brother Bardiya before the Egyptian campaign to prevent a rival claim to the throne.

- In March 522 BCE, a man claiming to be Bardiya led a rebellion, exploiting unrest and potential economic hardships.

- Cambyses died in July 522 BCE without suppressing the revolt, leaving the empire in turmoil.

- Darius I, later king, was involved in the imperial administration during this crucial period.

The reign of Cambyses is a study in the gap between conquest and consolidation. Winning Egypt was a significant achievement; maintaining an empire across vast lands while managing succession, loyalty, and economic strain was an entirely different challenge. That challenge fell to Darius I - a challenge that would define the Achaemenid Empire for generations.

Chapter 5
Darius I - Empire Builder

He seized power amid a crisis, with the empire fracturing and rivals near. Within a decade, he transformed chaos into the largest empire the world had yet seen. Darius I was not born to rule Persia -he fought his way to the throne and spent his reign proving he deserved it.

His story is among the most remarkable in the ancient world: a man who transformed political survival into institutional genius, rebuilding a near-collapsed kingdom into something so well-organized that its structures outlasted him by centuries. To understand the Persian Empire at its height - its roads, taxes, governors, and coins - you must understand Darius.

He reigned from 522 to 486 BCE, reshaping the ancient Near East in those 36 years. What he built was not just a military empire but a functioning state, with standardized systems, delegated authority, and revolutionary governance for its time.

The Struggle for the Throne

Power in the ancient world rarely transferred smoothly. When Darius came to power in 522 BCE, it was after a succession crisis had left the Achaemenid dynasty vulnerable.

The chaos began with Cambyses II's death, son of Cyrus the Great.

In the confusion, Gaumata - described in Darius's inscriptions as a pretender falsely claiming to be Cambyses's murdered brother Smerdis - seized the throne. Whether Gaumata was truly an impostor remains debated. What followed was clear.

Darius, a member of the Achaemenid royal family and high-ranking officer, led Persian nobles in conspiring against Gaumata. They killed him in 522 BCE, and Darius took the throne.

Yet, killing a rival and consolidating power are different. Rebellions erupted across the empire. Subject peoples who had tolerated Persian rule under Cyrus and Cambyses saw an opportunity. Babylon revolted. Media revolted. Egypt grew restless. Pretenders claiming royal blood appeared in various provinces, each a potential rallying point for dissent.

What followed was less a reign than a military campaign to create one. Darius fought battle after battle. His inscriptions at Behistun, carved into a cliff in present-day western Iran, record nineteen battles and the defeat of nine rebel kings in a single year. The Behistun Inscription, written in Old Persian, Elamite, and Babylonian, is crucial, commissioned by Darius to tell his version of events to anyone who could read - and to the gods he claimed sanctioned his rule.

He understood military victory alone wouldn't secure legitimacy. He needed a narrative, and he crafted one.

Making the Case for Divine Right

At Behistun, Darius presented himself not as a usurper but a restorer - chosen by Ahura Mazda, the supreme Zoroastrian deity, to rescue the empire from a fraud. Gaumata was the deceiver; Darius was the truth-teller. This framing was intentional - a political theology recasting a coup as divine correction.

He repeated this message across the empire through inscriptions, architecture, and religious patronage, positioning himself as the legitimate heir to Cyrus the Great's legacy - rightful continuation of a dynasty briefly usurped by an impostor. Whether his audiences fully believed is uncertain, but the message was consistent, persistent, and backed by military force.

By around 520 BCE, major rebellions were suppressed. Darius stood as undisputed ruler of an empire stretching from the Aegean coast to the Indus Valley, from Central Asia's steppes to Egypt's deserts. He hadn't inherited this empire intact; he reconquered it, demonstrating the ruthless competence ancient empires demanded of rulers.

Now came the harder work: governing it.

Reorganizing an Empire

Ruling such a vast territory - diverse in language, religion, culture, and geography - required more than military dominance. Cyrus had been a brilliant conqueror with a gift for tolerance. Darius was different: a builder of systems.

His most significant reform was reorganizing the empire into administrative units called satrapies. Each was governed by a satrap - derived from Old Persian for "protector of the kingdom." These weren't local chieftains or hereditary rulers operating independently.

Satrapies reported directly to Darius, collected taxes on his behalf, maintained order in his name, and were subject to inspection by royal officials - the "eyes and ears of the king" - who traveled the empire ensuring compliance and rooting out corruption.

This model of delegated authority was sophisticated. Darius recognized he couldn't personally manage every corner of the empire. So, he created a layer of trusted governors to extend his reach, while retaining mechanisms to check their power. Satraps held real authority but were never fully autonomous, with accountability running upward to Darius himself.

Expansion and Consolidation

While reorganizing administrative structures, Darius also expanded the empire. He incorporated parts of the Indus Valley - modern-day Pakistan and northwestern India - bringing new wealth to the imperial treasury. He pushed north into Central Asia and west toward Europe, launching a campaign into Scythian territory, though less successful than his eastern conquests.

In Egypt, already part of the empire, Darius's administration stabilized and integrated it more fully. Egyptian sources remember him with unusual warmth for a foreign ruler - possibly reflecting his respect for local religious traditions and presenting himself as a legitimate pharaoh rather than an occupier.

This pattern - military expansion combined with cultural accommodation - was a hallmark of Achaemenid rule, refined by Darius into a governing philosophy.

Subject peoples were generally allowed to maintain their religions, customs, and elites, provided they paid taxes and kept peace. It was pragmatic tolerance, not idealism, but it worked.

Building the Infrastructure of Power

An empire from Egypt to India needed more than intentions to hold together. Darius understood this, heavily investing in physical and institutional infrastructure enabling communication and control across vast distances.

His celebrated project, the Royal Road - about 1,500 miles from Sardis to Susa - had relay stations with fresh horses and riders. Royal couriers could traverse it in days - a speed nearly miraculous to contemporaries. Herodotus, the Greek historian, wrote of these couriers: "Neither snow nor rain nor heat nor darkness of night prevents these couriers from completing their designated stages with utmost speed."

This phrase later became the unofficial motto of the United States Postal Service - a testament to Darius's organizational innovations echoing through history.

Standardization: The Architecture of a Functioning State

Perhaps the most underappreciated aspect of Darius's reign was his drive toward standardization. Empires relying solely on force are brittle; those with common systems - of measurement, currency, and law - develop resilience outlasting individual rulers.

Darius introduced a standardized coinage system, with the gold daric and silver siglos as standard currencies, simplifying trade and tax collection across the empire. Every coin, bearing the king's image, was imperial propaganda.

He standardized weights and measures across the empire, reducing commercial friction between regions with different traditions. He promoted Aramaic as the administrative language - a practical choice, as it was a widely spoken trade language. A common language meant royal decrees, tax records, and correspondence could move across the empire without requiring translation.

These reforms - satrapies, the Royal Road, coinage, common language - amounted to a deliberate attempt at creating the institutional architecture of a functioning state, not merely a collection of conquered peoples held by force.

Legacy & Long-Term Impact

Darius I died in 486 BCE, leaving behind an empire at its power peak and an administrative framework defining Persian governance for generations. His successors inherited not just territory but a system, sophisticated enough to survive weak rulers and military setbacks.

His influence extended beyond Persia. The administrative models he developed influenced later empires, including those of Alexander the Great's successors, who adapted Achaemenid structures. Provincial governance through appointed officials answerable to central authority echoed through the Roman Empire and beyond.

Darius also left a physical legacy. His building projects at Persepolis, the great ceremonial capital he began around 518 BCE, produced stunning monumental architecture. The ruins, in modern Iran, feature carved reliefs showing delegations from across the empire bringing tribute to the Persian king - a visual record of the world Darius built.

Quick Summary

- Darius I reigned from 522 to 486 BCE, considered the greatest administrator of the Achaemenid Empire.

- He seized power after defeating Gaumata, a pretender, and suppressed widespread rebellions across the empire.

- His Behistun Inscription served as both historical record and political legitimation, framing his rule as divinely sanctioned.

- He reorganized the empire into satrapies, with governors reporting directly to him and subject to royal inspection.

- Darius expanded the empire east to the Indus Valley, west toward Europe, and consolidated Persian control over Egypt.

- The Royal Road enabled rapid communication across the empire.

- He introduced standardized coinage, weights and measures, and Aramaic as the administrative language.

- These reforms created an institutional framework outlasting Darius and influencing future empires.

What Darius built was essentially a wager on organization over brute force - an empire held together by systems, not fear. For a time, that bet paid off spectacularly. The world he shaped didn't unravel until a young Macedonian king arrived with ambitions to match his own.

PART 3
HOW THE EMPIRE WORKED

Chapter 6
Satrapies and Provincial Rule

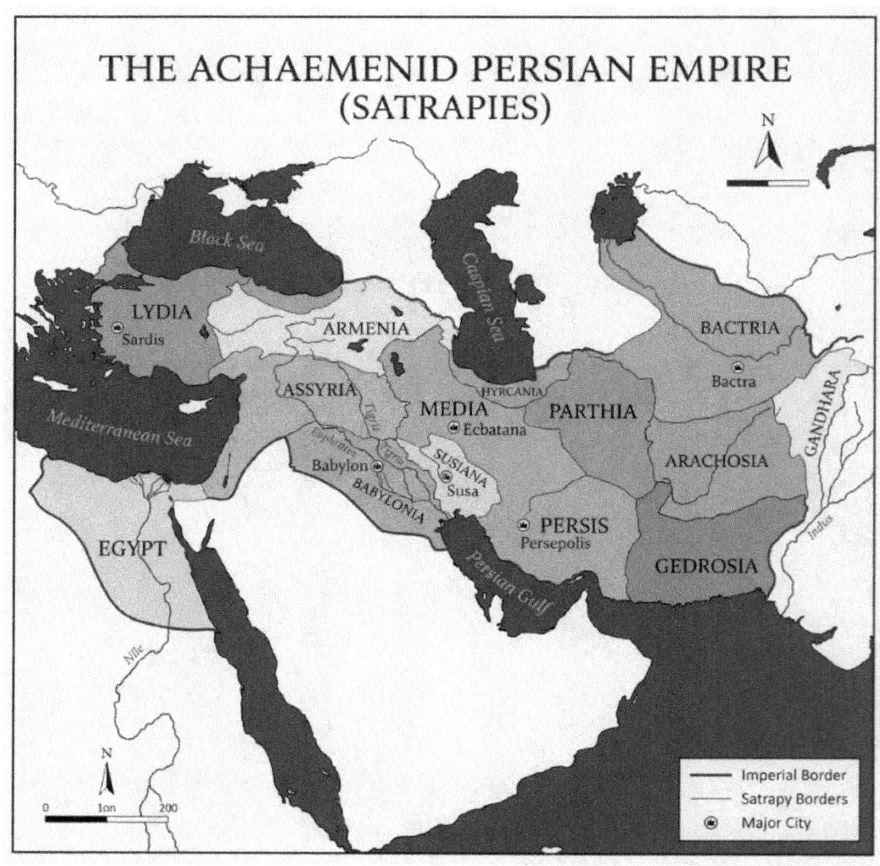

Satrapy Divisions Map

The Persian king Darius I ruled an empire that stretched from the Aegean coast to the Indus River - a domain so vast that no single man, court, or city could possibly govern it alone. The solution devised by his dynasty was one of the ancient world's most sophisticated administrative experiments: a system of provincial rule that balanced imperial authority with local autonomy, uniting peoples of diverse languages, customs, and loyalties under a single crown.

An Empire Too Large to Hold in One Fist

Governing such an expansive territory was not simply a logistical challenge; it was a philosophical one. How could the loyalty of a Babylonian merchant, a Greek coastal city, and a tribal confederation on the edge of the Indian subcontinent be maintained simultaneously, without a modern bureaucracy? How were taxes collected from populations never met, in currencies and commodities perhaps never seen?

The Achaemenid solution was the satrapy: a provincial unit administered by a governor called a satrap, drawn from the Persian nobility and answerable directly to the king. At its height, the empire was divided into roughly twenty to thirty provinces, each a semi-autonomous world. The satrap was not merely an administrator; he was a viceroy - a representative of royal power, expected to project the king's authority while managing the realities of his territory.

This chapter examines how that system worked in practice, how the empire kept its satraps in check, and how local elites across the empire - from Mesopotamia to the Indus Valley - became essential partners in making Persian rule function.

The Satrap: Governor, General, and Royal Proxy

The Office and Its Responsibilities

A satrap's duties were comprehensive and demanding. He oversaw tax collection, managed trade routes, maintained order, administered justice, and raised troops when needed. In a pre-modern empire without telecommunications or rapid transport, the satrap effectively embodied the empire in his province. His decisions shaped daily life for millions who would never see Persepolis.

Tax collection was perhaps the most consequential of these responsibilities. Each satrapy was assessed a fixed tribute, paid in silver or in-kind, which flowed to the royal treasury. Herodotus, writing in the fifth century BCE, recorded the tribute assessments for many provinces. The Hindush satrapy, encompassing the Indus Valley, was among the wealthiest, contributing 360 talents of gold dust, reflecting the region's extraordinary productivity.

Beyond taxation, satraps managed the empire's road network and oversaw the movement of goods. Trade routes were not merely economic lifelines; they were instruments of political integration. A satrap who kept roads safe and commerce flowing maintained a stable province.

Appointment and Social Standing

Satraps were typically drawn from the Persian aristocracy, often from the Achaemenid royal family. This ensured that the satrapy system reinforced dynastic loyalty rather than undermining it. A rebellious satrap was a disloyal official and a family member turning against his own.

Satrapal revolts did occur, especially in the fourth century BCE when central authority weakened. However, the system's social architecture created strong incentives for compliance. A satrap's wealth and prestige depended on his standing within the imperial order, with defection carrying not just political risk but social annihilation.

The Hindush Satrapy: The Empire's Eastern Edge

Among the remarkable Achaemenid satrapies was Hindush, established after Darius I's campaigns into the Indus Valley in the late sixth century BCE. Here, the empire encountered a region of river-fed plains, dense trade networks, and deep cultural traditions distinct from those of the Iranian plateau.

Administering Hindush required adaptation. The satrapal structure was tailored to local practices and elites, creating a form of governance that was recognizably Achaemenid but regionally distinct - a pattern repeated wherever Persian rule encountered deeply rooted local cultures.

Achaemenid presence in Hindush endured until the late fourth century BCE when Alexander the Great's campaigns dismantled the empire's eastern provinces. However, the administrative legacy of the satrapy persisted, influencing the governance structures of subsequent empires.

Watching the Watchers: Oversight and Control

The King's Eyes and Ears

Delegating authority to powerful provincial governors posed a clear problem: preventing satraps from becoming too powerful or corrupt. The Achaemenids developed mechanisms to address this.

Most famous was the royal inspector, known as the "King's Eye" or "King's Ear." These officials conducted audits, investigated complaints, and reported back to the court. Their visits were unannounced, their authority royal, and their findings could end careers or lives.

The empire also maintained separate military commanders in many satrapies, independent of the satrap. This deliberate division of civil and military power acted as a check on any single official's authority. Separating these functions meant that conspiracy required coordination, which left traces.

Infrastructure as Surveillance

Control also operated through infrastructure. The Royal Road, connecting Susa to Sardis over roughly 2,700 kilometers, was more than a trade route; it was a communication system. Royal couriers could traverse it swiftly, allowing the king to remain connected to his provinces.

This capacity for rapid communication meant that the king was never entirely absent from his provinces, despite the distances. A wayward satrap could expect a royal response faster than he might anticipate.

Local Elites and the Art of Cooperation

Why Local Partners Were Indispensable

No imperial system can function through coercion alone. The Achaemenids understood this clearly. Across the empire, they cultivated relationships with local elites - priests, merchants, tribal leaders, and nobles - whose cooperation was essential.

In Babylonia, the Achaemenids respected temple institutions and maintained local religious practices. In Egypt, they adopted the iconography and obligations of pharaohs. In the Indus Valley, they worked with tribal confederations, incorporating their leaders into the imperial structure.

Tribal Confederations and the Limits of Direct Rule

Figures like Madates, a leader of tribal confederations, illustrate this dynamic. In regions where direct control was impractical, the Achaemenids governed through intermediaries.

This pragmatism converted potential resistance into managed cooperation. A tribal confederation that collected tribute and maintained peace was of greater value than military occupation. By making local leaders partners, the Achaemenids turned potential opponents into stakeholders.

This arrangement carried risks. A powerful local elite could become a source of instability. Managing these relationships required political intelligence, cultivated by the best satraps for survival.

The Long Shadow of Achaemenid Practice

When Alexander's campaigns ended Achaemenid rule in the east, and the Mauryan Empire subsequently rose, the administrative legacy of Persian governance did not vanish. The Mauryans adapted Persian methods of provincial oversight and revenue collection.

This was more than direct copying; it was the absorption of practical knowledge on governing large, diverse territories. The experience under satrapal governance influenced how subsequent rulers approached provincial control.

Legacy & Long-Term Impact

The satrapy system's enduring contribution was not a specific institution but a set of principles: that large empires require delegated authority; that delegation requires oversight; and that sustainable rule depends on cooperation with local elites.

While not uniquely Persian insights, the Achaemenids applied them across diverse territories with sophistication. The empire endured for over two centuries, governing a significant portion of the world's population.

The Hindush satrapy illustrates the reach and limits of this system. Persian rule transformed the Indus Valley's global connection but adapted to existing realities, proving adaptability to be the system's greatest strength and longest-lasting legacy.

Quick Summary

- **The satrapy system** divided the Achaemenid Empire into about twenty to thirty provinces, each governed by a satrap overseeing taxation, trade, justice, and military affairs.

- **Satraps were drawn from the Persian nobility**, often reinforcing dynastic loyalty.

- **The Hindush satrapy** was one of the empire's wealthiest, assessed at 360 talents of gold dust.

- **Oversight included royal inspectors**, separate military commanders, and the rapid communication system of the Royal Road.

- **Local elites were crucial partners** - priests, merchants, and tribal leaders like Madates were integrated into the imperial structure.

- **Tribal confederations** acted as intermediaries in regions where direct control was impractical, converting resistance into cooperation.

- **Achaemenid practices influenced the Mauryan Empire**, which adapted Persian methods of governance.

- **The system's core insight** - that sustainable empire requires delegated authority, structured oversight, and local cooperation - shaped regional statecraft for generations.

What the Achaemenids built was more than a tax-collection mechanism or a military occupation; it was a theory of empire acknowledging the limits of central power and transforming them into resilience.

When Alexander advanced and the Persian court at Persepolis burned, the administrative habits of two centuries lived on. They endured in the officials, elites, and peoples who knew no other governance, and who, in time, taught their conquerors how to rule.

Chapter 7
Roads, Communication, and Scale

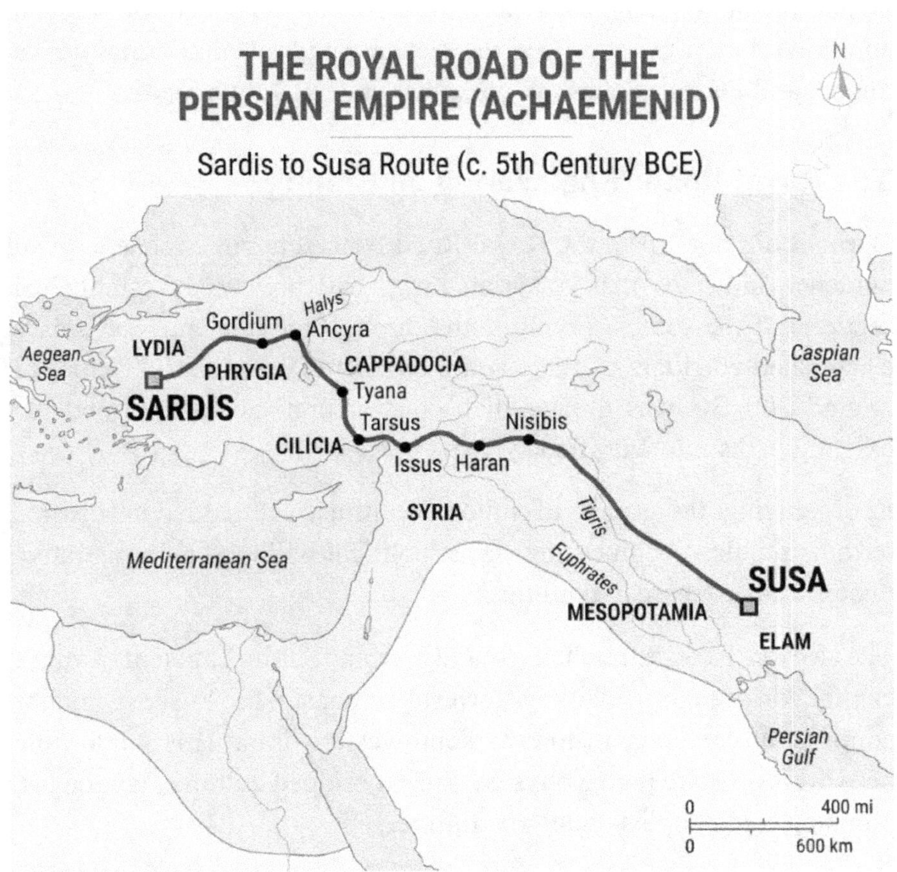

The Royal Road

An empire is only as strong as its slowest message. When rebellion erupts on a distant frontier, when treachery brews, or when an army awaits orders, the survival of an empire hinges not just on *what* is known, but *how fast* it is known. The Achaemenid Persian Empire, sprawling from the Aegean coast to Central Asia's edge, grasped this truth. Around 500 BC, under Darius I, they developed a solution of remarkable clarity.

Darius expanded the Royal Road: a vast highway system that was essential for governing one of the ancient world's largest empires. Greek historians marveled at it, merchants depended on it, and administrators used it to keep the Achaemenid machine running. To understand Persia's cohesion, one must understand its roads.

The Royal Road: Engineering an Empire

Darius I did not create the Royal Road from scratch. Archaeological evidence indicates that Assyrian kings had previously established sections of the route, carving paths through the ancient Near East's established corridors of trade and movement. What Darius achieved around 500 BC was greater than construction: he transformed the existing paths into a unified system.

Reorganizing thousands of miles of infrastructure across diverse terrains required engineering skills, political will, and administrative vision. Darius possessed all three.

The Royal Road stretched roughly from Sardis, ancient Lydia's capital on modern Turkey's western coast, to Susa, a major administrative center in today's southwestern Iran. This 1,600-mile network was more than a physical link; it bridged cultures, languages, climates, and peoples under one throne.

Built for Speed, Not Comfort

The Royal Road's innovation lay in its design for rapid communication. The Persian administration installed relay stations along the route, where fresh horses and riders awaited. A royal messenger didn't exhaust a single horse over the road's entire length but relayed messages from station to station.

This system achieved remarkable speeds for the time.

Couriers could cover the entire road in approximately nine days. In stark contrast, regular travelers took about three months. This nine-day gap was pivotal - the difference between an empire responsive to crises and one unable to act.

The Greek historian Herodotus depicted this system with admiration: *"Neither snow, nor rain, nor heat, nor darkness of night prevents these couriers from completing their designated stages with utmost speed."* Whether quoting an official Persian description or recording his own observations, the sentiment highlights the road's impressive efficiency. This phrase has echoed through history, eventually aligning, albeit loosely, with modern postal mottos.

A Road Through the Western Empire

It's crucial to note that the Royal Road primarily served the Achaemenid Empire's western territories. While Susa was a central hub, the road focused on regions stretching towards the Mediterranean - areas recently incorporated and culturally diverse, posing significant governance challenges. Darius prioritized fast communication where his control was newest and most contested.

The road connected to wider trade networks that extended eastward, including routes later known as the Silk Road. Merchants, diplomats, and travelers used these paths, carrying not only goods but also ideas, languages, and cultural practices. The Royal Road was the empire's administrative backbone but also a channel for interaction among civilizations.

The Postal System: Relay, Trust, and Control

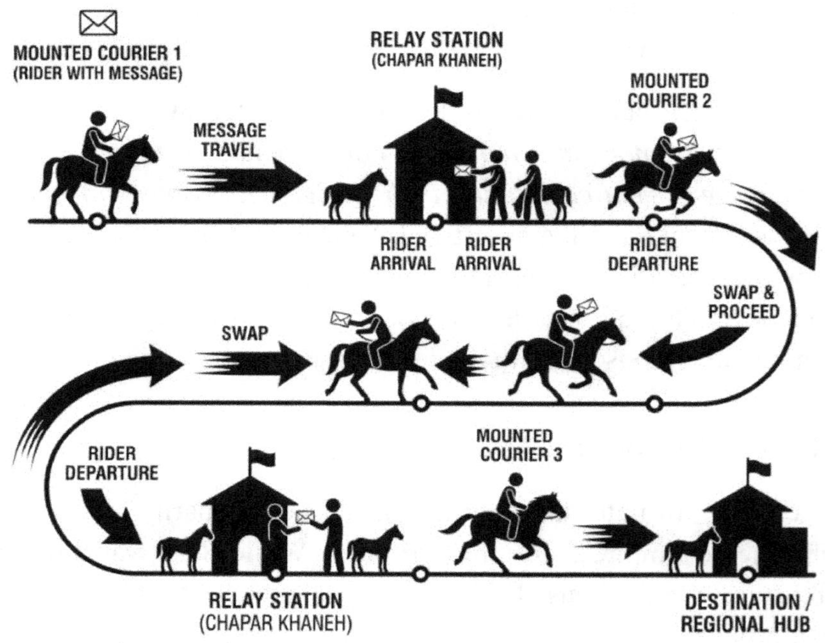

Postal Relay System

The relay stations weren't mere rest stops; they formed the ancient world's most advanced postal system, requiring organization, resources, and trust.

Each station needed staffing, supply, and maintenance. Proper management ensured smooth handoffs and verified messengers' credentials, safeguarding communication integrity. In an empire where a forged message could provoke disastrous actions, reliability and speed were paramount.

The postal network primarily served the crown, facilitating royal decrees, military orders, and intelligence reports. It wasn't a public service in the modern sense; it was an imperial tool. However, it allowed information flow, enabling governors and local officials to communicate with the center, integrating the administrative network.

The Architecture of Administration

The postal system addressed a fundamental large-scale governance challenge: maintaining control over distant territories.

Distance in the ancient world wasn't a mere inconvenience - it was a political threat. A governor too far to receive orders or send timely reports risked acting independently or making critical errors. The relay system bridged that distance, informing Susa of crises in Sardis within nine days, enabling timely responses.

Darius I saw empire governance as an information challenge. Roads and horses were his solution.

Imperial Connectivity: What Roads Make Possible

Beyond relay stations and couriers, a greater vision emerges. The Royal Road and its supporting postal system embodied an imperial concept.

An empire failing to communicate effectively is merely a set of territories under a ruler's name. It becomes a cohesive political entity through coordination of orders, resources, and information. Under Darius I, the Achaemenid Empire uniquely built infrastructure to achieve such coordination.

Trade, Culture, and the Road's Wider World

The Royal Road's connectivity extended beyond mere administration, having far-reaching cultural and economic effects. When roads exist, people are bound to use them - not only the king's messengers but merchants, pilgrims, soldiers, and wanderers. The road carried

Darius's decrees alongside Lydian silver, Babylonian textiles, Greek philosophies, and Zoroastrian beliefs.

Linking Sardis to Susa and broader trade networks, the Royal Road positioned the Achaemenid Empire as a crossroads for civilizations. Cultures that might have remained isolated met and mixed, languages intertwined, technologies spread, and religious ideas traveled. The road facilitated these interactions.

Cohesion and Stability

Historians attribute the Achaemenid Empire's longevity to its infrastructure. The Royal Road was crucial in maintaining such a diverse empire. By facilitating rapid communication, it projected central authority outward. By linking trade routes, it provided economic incentives to stay within the imperial fold. By physically connecting distant regions, it fostered a sense of unity.

This cohesiveness wasn't absolute, as the empire faced rebellions and external pressures. Yet, the infrastructure Darius established contributed resilience that surpassed mere military strength.

Quick Summary

- Darius I reorganized the Royal Road around 500 BC, building upon Assyrian-established routes.

- Spanning approximately 1,600 miles, the road linked Sardis in the west to Susa in the east, crossing the Achaemenid heartland.

- A relay system allowed couriers to traverse the road in nine days, significantly faster than the three-month journey for ordinary travelers.

- Herodotus documented the road and its couriers, providing a lasting historical account of ancient postal systems.

- Primarily a tool of imperial governance, the postal system enabled swift communication between the center and distant provinces.

- The road was a conduit for cultural and commercial exchange, linking to early Silk Road corridors.

- Infrastructure was vital in maintaining imperial cohesion, extending beyond mere convenience.

Roads endure beyond the empires that construct them. Even after Darius and the Achaemenid Empire fell to Alexander, the routes they maintained continued serving travelers and traders. This longevity is a testament - not only to their quality but to the insight of their conception. Darius understood that power at scale travels on roads, a principle proven time and again by subsequent empires.

Chapter 8
Economy and Taxation

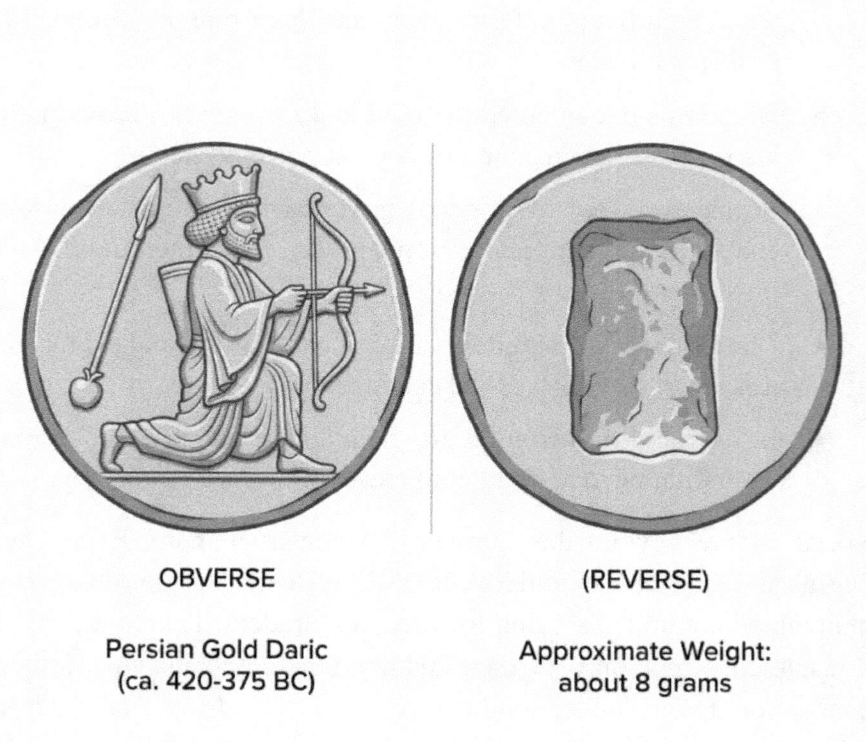

Persian Gold Coin (Daric)

The Roman Empire, at its height, stretched from the Scottish borderlands to the sands of Mesopotamia. Sustaining such a vast realm required more than legions and roads - it demanded substantial financial resources. Soldiers needed pay, fleets required funding, and governors commanded salaries. The empire's infrastructure, from aqueducts to amphitheaters, depended on continuous fiscal support. Understanding how Rome extracted, managed, and circulated its wealth reveals much about its resilience and eventual decline.

This chapter explores the economic foundations of the Roman world: the tribute system funneling resources to the center, the agricultural structures underpinning wealth, and the coinage and trade networks that linked distant provinces in a commercial web. Together, these systems formed the economic core of Roman civilization.

The Tribute System: Empire as Extraction Machine

Rome's conquests were driven by more than military ambition; they were also motivated by economic strategy. Upon absorbing new territories, Rome seized their productive capacities - farmland, mines, ports, and populations - imposing a tribute system. This systematic obligation required the conquered to finance their conquerors. While not unique to Rome, which refined the system with administrative precision, it was a critical tool of empire.

The Nature of Tribute

Tribute varied by province and era, commonly taking the form of *tributum soli*, a tax on land and produce. Landowners - whether Roman citizens, local elites, or subject farmers - paid a portion of their yield. Alongside this was the *tributum capitis*, a poll tax in the eastern provinces. Depending on the region, tribute could be paid in kind or monetized in coin. For many farmers, owing coin meant exposure to market fluctuations, adding economic strain.

Collection Mechanics

Initially, Rome rarely collected taxes directly, relying instead on *publicani*, private tax farmers who paid the treasury upfront and extracted taxes to reclaim their investment and profit. This incentivized exploitation, prompting imperial reforms that eventually replaced *publicani* with salaried officials. The intent was both humanitarian and practical, recognizing that impoverished populations were unsustainable for tax collection.

Provincial Variation and Local Elites

Not all provinces bore the same burden. Roman citizenship conferred tax privileges, and provincial elites often negotiated favorable terms in exchange for loyalty. Such arrangements integrated local elites into the imperial system, ensuring their cooperation without deploying extensive administrative resources.

Imperial Revenue Scale

Estimating Roman state revenue is challenging due to sparse records, but sources like Augustus' treasury summary offer insights. Provinces like Egypt, a key grain supplier, contributed vast resources. Tribute fueled Roman governance, impacting military funding and public welfare, making it central to Roman life.

Agriculture and Land: The Bedrock of Ancient Wealth

Agriculture was the cornerstone of Roman wealth. With economies rooted in agrarian practices, land served as primary capital, and farming was pivotal for prosperity.

Roman Landholding Structure

Land tenure ranged from small peasant farms to vast *latifundia*, large estates worked by enslaved labor. As conquests increased, these estates expanded, often at the expense of small farmers who migrated to cities, exacerbating urban poverty and triggering land redistribution crises.

Tenant Farming and the Colonate

Over time, tenant farming became prevalent. The *coloni* worked land owned by wealthy landlords in exchange for a portion of the harvest.

Although initially beneficial, legal restrictions eventually bound tenant farmers to the land, mirroring precursors to medieval serfdom.

Crops and Regional Specialization

Roman agriculture thrived on wheat, olives, and grapes, with regional specialization across Egypt, North Africa, Spain, and Gaul. This surplus supported a thriving trade network, a hallmark of the Roman economy.

Land as Status, Land as Power

For the Roman elite, land symbolized status and power. Although urban and commercial realities evolved, aristocratic ideals remained intertwined with agricultural traditions, emphasizing the cultural significance of landownership.

Coinage and Trade: The Arteries of Empire

While land produced wealth, coinage and trade circulated it. The Roman monetary system was a significant achievement, with standardized currency fostering economic transactions across vast distances.

Roman Monetary System

Coinage was hierarchically structured - gold *aureus*, silver *denarius*, and bronze *sestertius*. This system, maintained for centuries, facilitated diverse commercial activities. Coins functioned as both currency and political symbols, reinforcing imperial presence throughout the empire.

Debasement and Its Impact

Maintaining currency stability was crucial, yet emperors occasionally debased coinage due to fiscal pressures. This erosion of confidence led to inflation, contributing to the empire's later economic instability.

Trade Networks: Local and Long-Distance

Roman trade spanned local markets to global networks, extending to Africa, India, and China. Archaeological finds, such as shipwrecks and coin hoards, highlight these extensive connections and their role in shaping economic activity.

Merchants and Trade Stigma

Despite elite disdain for trade, commerce flourished through diverse participants, including freedmen and foreigners. These traders defied social stigmas, fostering a vibrant commercial environment across the Mediterranean and beyond.

Infrastructure and Legal Support

Rome's infrastructure supported trade, with roads facilitating military and commercial movement. The legal system developed robust frameworks for contracts and partnerships, reducing trade risks and ensuring economic stability.

Analysis: Interconnected Systems and Emerging Strains

Tribute, agriculture, and trade were interdependent, each sustaining the other. Agricultural productivity influenced taxation and trade, while coinage facilitated commerce. During times of prosperity, these systems supported the empire's unparalleled integration and growth.

However, structural vulnerabilities persisted. Dependency on military expansion, monetary stability challenges, and agricultural pressures foreshadowed eventual strains. By the third century CE, these pressures converged, testing the empire's economic fabric.

Key Takeaways

- Roman tribute systematically extracted wealth, primarily through land and poll taxes.

- Tax farming was curtailed by reforms, transitioning to salaried officials to limit exploitation.

- Agriculture underpinned wealth, with diverse land tenures and shifting labor dynamics influencing social structures.

- Coinage facilitated widespread commerce despite the risks of debasement and inflation.

- Roman trade networks extended globally, with merchants overcoming cultural stigmas to thrive.

Rome's economic prowess was intertwined with its political power, laying foundations that continued to shape the medieval world.

PART 4
POWER AND IDEOLOGY

Chapter 9
Kingship and the Court

At Persepolis, carved into the rock of a mountain cliff, Darius the Great left no doubt about the seat of power: "I am Darius the Great King," the inscription states, "King of Kings, King of countries containing all kinds of men, King of this great earth far and wide." This was not mere pride; it was a theological assertion.

Kingship in the Achaemenid Empire was more than a political arrangement; it was a declaration that heaven's order mirrored earth's, with the Persian king at the center. Understanding this ideology is crucial to comprehending how the ancient empire sustained itself across generations, languages, and vast territories.

This chapter explores the formidable ideology of Persian kingship, the court structures that converted royal authority into governance, and the volatile issue of succession — the empire's greatest strength was also its most perilous vulnerability.

The King of Kings: An Ideology Built to Last

The title *Shahanshah* - King of Kings - predates the Achaemenids, but they perfected its use. Under Darius, who ruled from 522 to 486 BCE, it became more than an honorific; it was the cornerstone of a political theology.

Being King of Kings meant ruling over rulers. The empire encompassed numerous subordinate kings and dynasts who submitted to Achaemenid power. The Persian king ruled both people and their leaders, a significant distinction that underscored the scale and model of governance.

The ideology transcended mere hierarchy. Achaemenid inscriptions, carved in Old Persian at sites like Behistun and Persepolis, cast the king as Ahura Mazda's chosen instrument, the supreme deity of Zoroastrianism. Darius did not claim to be divine but asserted that he was selected by the god of truth to bring justice and stability.

This perspective had practical implications. Following the death of Cambyses in 522 BCE, Darius quelled revolts not as military victories but as restorations of divine order against cosmic disorder - a compelling narrative that framed rebellion against him as both treason and impiety.

A Universal Monarch

Darius extended this ideology, presenting himself not as a Persian king ruling foreigners, but as a universal monarch whose legitimacy transcended ethnicity. His inscriptions list diverse peoples - Medes, Babylonians, Egyptians, and others - as integral parts of a divinely ordered whole.

This was politically astute. The Achaemenids absorbed rather than erased local cultures and traditions, portraying the king as each people's rightful ruler on their terms. In Egypt, he wore the pharaohs' double crown; in Babylon, he participated in their kingship rituals. The king became whatever the context demanded.

Darius' reforms reinforced this universalism by dividing the empire into satrapies, large administrative provinces each governed by a satrap. Royal inspectors, the "eyes and ears of the king," ensured the satraps remained loyal.

The ideology's physical expression was Persepolis, the ceremonial capital. Its Apadana hall, adorned with reliefs of tribute-bearing delegations, visually represented the notion that all roads and peoples led to the god-chosen king.

The Court: Power Behind the Throne

Behind divine kingship lay a complex court structure that transformed royal will into imperial reality and generated its own politics.

At the center was the royal household. The king's family, including wives and siblings, held politically charged positions. Royal women, such as the queen mother, wielded considerable influence, sometimes unseen in official records. The harem, far from a mere domestic space, was a political arena.

Surrounding the royal family were high nobles from Persian and Median aristocracy. These individuals commanded military, governed regions, and held courtly positions like cup-bearer and bodyguard commander. Proximity to the king equaled power.

The court was a place of spectacle. Audiences with the king followed strict protocols. Visitors prostrated, gift exchanges were formalized, and rank determined seating. All emphasized the king's status as a category beyond mere mortals.

An administrative class - scribes, officials, and logisticians - supported the court. The Persepolis Fortification Tablets, an archive from Darius' reign, reveal a sophisticated bureaucracy meticulously managing the empire's logistics.

The Dangerous Question of Succession

Despite its grandeur, the Achaemenid system's Achilles' heel was succession.

Persian kingship was hereditary, yet complex. Heirs were usually designated, with the chief queen's eldest son having a strong customary claim, but succession was fraught with crises.

The challenge was partly biological: large harems led to many sons and potential factions. Nobles, commanders, and royal women backed different princes, sometimes violently.

Darius' path to the throne was complex. Not a direct heir of Cambyses, his claim was a mix of lineage and military force against rivals in 522 BCE. His Behistun inscription worked to justify his legitimacy, indicating succession needed to be argued, not assumed.

Darius designated Xerxes as heir before his Egyptian campaign, acknowledging that royal authority required careful management. Succession was a continuous political project, demanding the court's alliances and influences be strategically aligned.

Legacy & Long-Term Impact

The Achaemenid kingship model proved enduring, influencing successor empires post-Alexander's conquest in the 330s BCE. The Seleucids, Parthians, and Sasanians all adapted elements of this template.

What made it durable was its flexibility. Grounding authority in a cosmic claim allowed the empire to expand and incorporate diverse peoples without requiring them to become Persian. The King of Kings served as a unifying figure for all subjects - a substantial political achievement.

Quick Summary

- Darius the Great reigned from 522 to 486 BCE, shaping Achaemenid ideology of kingship.

- The title "King of Kings" signified both the practical rule over rulers and a theological claim of divine selection.

- Achaemenid ideology framed opposition as cosmic disorder, equating rebellion with impiety.

- Darius organized the empire into satrapies to maintain authority across diverse regions.

- Persepolis symbolized Achaemenid universal kingship through its tribute depictions.

- The court comprised family, nobles, and administrators, with power linked directly to proximity to the king.

- Succession was vulnerable - multiple heirs fostered factional competition, demanding ongoing management.

- Darius secured Xerxes' succession, acknowledging that it required active construction.

Darius died around 486 BCE, leaving an expansive kingdom and an authoritative model that outlasted his dynasty. Yet, the court's dynamics and succession politics continued to shape the empire long after. How this system handled its greatest challenge is explored in the next chapter.

Chapter 10
Religion and Diversity

A king who conquers a city and then respects its gods is unusual. A king who funds the restoration of foreign temples, returns stolen idols, and declares himself a servant of foreign deities is rarer still. When Cyrus the Great entered Babylon in 539 BCE, he did precisely that.

What made such actions possible - and politically astute - was a religious framework the Persians had developed over generations. Zoroastrianism, one of the oldest monotheistic traditions, provided the Achaemenid kings with more than theology; it offered a governing philosophy. It defined their identity, cosmic obligations, and treatment of the ruled. In ancient Persia, religion was inseparable from politics - it was its foundation.

This chapter explores three interconnected dimensions: the role of Ahura Mazda in shaping royal ideology, the scholarly debate on the depth of Achaemenid Zoroastrianism, and the practical system of religious tolerance that allowed the empire to flourish across diverse cultures, languages, and faiths.

Ahura Mazda and the Language of Royal Power

Every Achaemenid king left inscriptions that invoked the name Ahura Mazda first, even before listing conquests. Darius I, ruling from 522 to 486 BCE, was particularly explicit. His Behistun inscription opens with the declaration that Ahura Mazda created the earth, sky, and humanity, and chose Darius as king.

This logic was necessary; Darius needed cosmic validation after seizing power during violent succession.

This invocation was not just decorative. It served an ideological function by placing the king within a moral order. In Zoroastrian theology, the universe is structured around the conflict between *asha* (truth, order) and *druj* (lie, chaos). A king favored by Ahura Mazda upheld *asha*. His enemies were agents of *druj*. Rebellion was not merely political but a cosmic offense.

Darius used this framework astutely. In the Behistun inscription, the nineteen kings he defeated are described as liars spreading *druj*. His victory is framed as a restoration of order. This religious language served a political purpose: it elevated Darius and delegitimized his challengers.

Xerxes, who ruled from 486 to 465 BCE, continued this tradition. His inscriptions echo his father's theological vocabulary, suggesting the Ahura Mazda formula had become a stable element of royal identity.

The empire's landscape reinforced this message. Fire temples, where the sacred flame was maintained, were architectural expressions of royal piety. Fire, in Zoroastrian belief, was not merely symbolic but a manifestation of divine light. When kings built and maintained these temples, they demonstrated their commitment to the cosmic order justifying their rule.

The Zoroastrian Debate

Historians disagree on whether these kings were fully Zoroastrian. Did they follow Zarathustra's teachings, or use Zoroastrian imagery selectively?

The evidence complicates this question. Royal inscriptions are propaganda, intended to shape public perception rather than reflect personal belief.

Cyrus the Great's behavior adds complexity. He's celebrated for religious tolerance, yet his inscriptions lack saturated Zoroastrian language. In Babylon, he presented himself as Marduk's servant. Was he a pragmatist adapting to contexts, or was Zoroastrianism not yet dominant during his reign?

Darius and Xerxes are a different puzzle. Their rhetoric is unmistakable, yet they also patronized non-Zoroastrian institutions. Xerxes' association with the destruction of Babylonian temples is interpreted variably - as religious intolerance or political punishment.

The most defensible position suggests the Achaemenid kings were influenced by Zoroastrian theology but were also pragmatic. Their religion provided moral vocabulary and cosmic legitimacy but allowed respectful engagement with other gods.

A System of Religious Tolerance

Regardless of personal convictions, Achaemenid kings built something remarkable for the ancient world: an empire that permitted subjects to worship their own gods.

This was strategic policy.

Cyrus set the precedent. Upon conquering Babylon, he restored local deities' statues and fulfilled Marduk's will, transforming potential resistance into cooperation. The Babylonian priestly class had every reason to support a king respecting their institutions.

His treatment of the Jewish community followed similar logic. Cyrus allowed Jewish exiles to return to Jerusalem and rebuild their Temple, earning him the title *mashiach* in the Hebrew Bible. For the Jewish community, Cyrus was an instrument of divine providence.

Achaemenid tolerance was not passive indifference but active engagement. Temples were centers of community identity and loyalty. Supporting them secured cooperation; destroying them invited rebellion.

Darius I formalized this approach across the empire. Local religious customs continued in the satrapies. The empire demanded taxes and loyalty, not theological conformity.

This tolerance had philosophical roots in Zoroastrianism, which emphasized *asha* - truth and justice. The religion did not require conversion for cosmic order. Kings could respect others' gods without compromising their own beliefs.

The interaction between Persian culture and the Jewish community is a key example. Persian support for the Jerusalem Temple influenced post-exilic Judaism. Structural parallels between Zoroastrian theology and later Jewish, Christian, and Islamic ideas illustrate the potential influence within the Achaemenid world.

Key Takeaways

- Zoroastrianism was the ideological language through which Achaemenid kings claimed legitimacy and defined their cosmic role.

- Ahura Mazda appears prominently in royal inscriptions, framing the king's authority as divinely sanctioned.

- Darius I used Zoroastrian concepts of truth (*asha*) and lie (*druj*) to delegitimize rivals and frame his rule as restoring cosmic order.

- Scholars debate how doctrinally Zoroastrian the kings were, noting Cyrus's adoption of other religious idioms.

- Achaemenid religious tolerance was a deliberate policy—kings supported the religious institutions of subject peoples.

- Cyrus's permission for Jewish exiles to rebuild the Temple illustrates how Persian policy affected other faiths' histories.

- Zoroastrian concepts may have influenced the development of later Abrahamic religions through contact within the Achaemenid empire.

Achaemenid kings built the largest empire of their time, uniting diverse peoples not through religious uniformity but through an ideology valuing order and justice. Ahura Mazda demanded truth and righteousness, leaving room for Babylonian priests, Jewish exiles, and others to coexist. This legacy is profound. The next inquiry explores how this world eventually unraveled and what it left behind.

PART 5
SOCIETY AND DAILY LIFE

Chapter 11
Women in the Persian Empire

Buried beneath the ruins of Persepolis, sealed within clay tablets that survived because Alexander the Great's soldiers inadvertently baked them in 330 BCE, lies remarkable evidence about women's lives in the ancient world. These are not legends or myths but actual administrative records - ration lists, wage documents, and travel authorizations - that reveal women as workers, supervisors, managers, and landowners across the Achaemenid Empire.

While most ancient civilizations left behind stories about women, Persia left behind the receipts.

What the Tablets Tell Us

In the 1930s, archaeologists excavating Persepolis uncovered tens of thousands of clay tablets dating from 509 to 494 BCE. Written in Elamite script, these documents - known as the Fortification Tablets and the Treasury Texts - were the empire's paperwork: the day-to-day records of an enormous administrative machine tracking allocations and transactions.

Extraordinary for their scope, these records list women among workers receiving rations of grain, wine, and beer - not as dependents or footnotes, but as named individuals paid for their labor. Women appear throughout the tablets in various roles, from laborers to supervisors. Some women received higher allocations, suggesting a hierarchy of skill or responsibility. Women who had recently given birth received supplemental rations, indicating a system attentive to their needs.

This was not marginal. Women appear across multiple sites and categories of work, indicating their economic participation was routine, not exceptional.

Travel, Authority, and Sealed Orders

One striking feature of the Fortification Tablets is the evidence of women's mobility. Travel rations - allocations for official travel - were recorded for women as well as men. Some women traveled with their own retinues, suggesting positions of genuine authority.

Royal women particularly stand out. The tablets document rations for the wives, mothers, and daughters of Persian kings as they managed households and operations afar. These were not mere ceremonial figures but active administrators.

Sealed orders add another layer. In the ancient Near East, a sealed document had legal weight. Women in the Achaemenid system issued such orders, directing economic activities and asserting control over resources. The seal symbolized power, and women wielded it.

Royal Women and the Management of Estates

Among the elite, Persian women's economic authority is most visible in estate management. Royal women - king's mothers, wives, daughters - administered landholdings, controlled workforces, and oversaw revenues. This was active management: orders, accounts, and agents were part of their domain.

The king's mother held a particularly notable position, appearing alongside the king's wife in inscriptions, highlighting her role beyond the domestic sphere. Funerary customs reinforced this status, marking royal women as significant in the imperial order.

The infrastructure of agents enabled elite women to manage estates through a network of subordinates issuing rations and representing their interests. While husbands sometimes assisted, research is clear that these estates belonged to the women, a distinction that set Achaemenid Persia apart.

Beyond the Palace: Non-Royal Women in the Economy

The Fortification Tablets document more than royal women - they reveal the economic lives of ordinary women. Female workers received wages and rations similar to their male counterparts, participating in food production, textile manufacture, and other central industries. Some women held supervisory roles, reflected by higher rations.

While these tablets don't reveal personal experiences, they show that the Achaemenid administration treated women as economic actors with valuable labor and real authority.

This is significant. In many ancient societies, women appear primarily through the actions of men. In the Persepolis tablets, they appear as they were.

What This Means: Interpreting the Evidence

Historians approach the Persepolis evidence cautiously. Administrative records showing women with wages and authority do not imply equality or freedom by modern standards. They reflect specific institutional contexts and may not represent all of Persian society.

However, the evidence highlights significant female economic participation in the Achaemenid framework. Women from royal to laboring classes appear as recognized participants in economic life, documented in the empire's records.

Funerary and inscriptional evidence reinforces this picture for elite women. The Achaemenid state did not merely tolerate women's economic activity; it incorporated it into imperial life.

Scholars note that the rights and roles available to women in this era were meaningful within their context. The Persepolis tablets do not depict a modern feminist ideal but rather a complex system where women's economic roles were substantial.

Legacy & Long-Term Impact

When Alexander's forces burned Persepolis in 330 BCE, they ended the Achaemenid Empire and preserved its records. The tablets offer historians a window into a world that might have been lost, including the lives of Persian women.

This challenges assumptions about ancient women as confined or invisible. Persian women, royal and non-royal, managed resources, issued orders, and received wages. They were economically active in ways that cannot be ignored.

Quick Summary

- **The Persepolis Fortification Tablets** (509-494 BCE) reveal women's economic roles in the Achaemenid Empire in detail.

- **Female workers** are documented as individuals receiving rations and wages, even in supervisory roles.

- **Women with newborns** received supplemental rations, reflecting attention to their unique needs.

- **Royal women** managed estates, issued orders, and traveled on official business, demonstrating genuine authority.

- **The king's mother and wife** were formally recognized, highlighting their status.

- **Elite women's estates** belonged to them, with husbands assisting but not owning.

- **The tablets show women as economic actors**, though broader social conditions remain unexplained.

- **Records preserved by Alexander's fire** provide direct insights into Persian women's lives.

What the Persepolis tablets ultimately offer is a reminder that the past was more varied, and women's roles more complex, than some narratives suggest. The Achaemenid Empire was not modern, and its women were not contemporary, but they were present, active, and consequential, as the clay record compellingly demonstrates.

Chapter 12
Everyday Life in the Empire

Rome was not built in a day - but it was run daily by countless individuals whose names never made it into the history books.

When most think of ancient Rome, they picture emperors, senators, gladiators, and legions. Yet, the empire that Augustus began constructing in 27 BCE was sustained by something more ordinary: bakers starting fires before dawn, scribes copying documents by lamplight, farmers coaxing grain from Italian soil, and merchants haggling across extensive trade routes. The grandeur of Rome rested on people living lives shaped by work, family, neighborhood, and the rhythms of where they happened to live.

This chapter moves away from the battlefield and Senate floor to explore daily Roman life during the empire's peak. It examines the workers and administrators who kept civilization running, the contrasts between city and countryside, and the remarkable cultural diversity that made the Roman Empire unlike any other in the ancient world.

Workers and Administrators: The Engine of Empire

Each morning across the Roman Empire, millions awoke to work - a simple fact that underpinned Roman power.

At the top of the administrative structure sat the emperor and his officials, managing an empire stretching from Britain to Egypt. Augustus, who transformed Rome from a republic into an empire after 27 BCE, recognized that governing such a vast territory required more than military force. It demanded bureaucracy - a class of administrators, record-keepers, tax collectors, and legal officials projecting Roman authority into every province, city, and village.

These administrators ranged from senior officials managing entire provinces to local clerks processing grain shipments or recording transactions. Many were freedmen - formerly enslaved individuals granted freedom - who found in imperial service a path to status and prosperity. Literacy, numeracy, and organizational skill were their essential tools, and the empire rewarded these skills.

Below the administrative class was a vast working population. Urban Rome was bustling with craftsmen, traders, and laborers. Potters, metalworkers, tanners, weavers, and construction workers filled the city's neighborhoods, organized into *collegia* - associations functioning as trade guilds, social clubs, and mutual aid societies. These groups provided workers with collective identity and practical support in times of need.

However, the Roman economy posed a fundamental tension for free workers as it relied significantly on slave labor. Enslaved people worked in mines, on farms, in workshops, and in wealthy households - receiving no wages and often undercutting the earning power of free workers. Urban plebeian laborers faced competition from enslaved workers performing the same tasks for nothing. This daily reality shaped wages, limited opportunities, and created a precarious existence for the working class.

The Forum Romanum was the center of Rome's economic and social world. More than a political space, the Forum was where business was conducted, legal disputes were argued, and social connections were maintained. Standing in the Forum meant standing at the intersection of commerce, law, and public life - a reminder that these elements were never separate in Rome.

Household work added complexity to this picture. In families wealthy enough to own enslaved people, household labor - cooking, cleaning, childcare, textile production - fell largely to enslaved workers. This harsh reality, however, created opportunities for women in such households: time for intellectual engagement, social activity, and cultural participation - opportunities unavailable to women in poorer households where survival required everyone's involvement.

Roman society was deeply patriarchal, yet within its rigid hierarchies, women navigated spaces of influence and agency, particularly in the domestic sphere and among elite women in the social networks shaping political life.

Urban vs. Rural Life: Two Worlds, One Empire

Rome the city and Rome the empire were distinctly different experiences of the same civilization.

Urban life in major cities - Rome, Carthage, Alexandria, Antioch - was dense, loud, and social. Apartment buildings, or *insulae*, rose several stories high, packing people into small areas. Ground-floor units were more desirable and expensive; upper floors, cheaper, more dangerous, and prone to fires and collapses that periodically devastated neighborhoods. For most urban residents, private space was limited. Life extended outward - into streets, public baths, markets, and temples.

Public baths, or *thermae*, were significant social institutions. Beyond cleanliness, they were gathering spots where people of different social classes mixed, gossiped, made deals, and spent leisure hours. Admission was affordable, sometimes free. In a city where private homes offered little comfort or space, the baths provided a genuinely democratic shared public life.

Rural life operated at a different pace. The Roman countryside was dominated by agriculture, and the agricultural calendar governed life. Planting and harvest seasons structured the year; the rhythms of livestock, weather, and soil determined routines independent of political dramas in the capital. Farmers lived lives of hardship and uncertainty, whether working small plots or laboring on large estates known as *latifundia*.

The *latifundia* system, relying heavily on enslaved labor, concentrated land ownership among elites and squeezed out many small farmers. Displaced farmers often drifted to cities, swelling the urban poor and intensifying competition for work.

Rural life, however, was not without social texture. Villages had festivals, local temples, and networks of mutual support. The Pax Romana - the long peace and stability initiated by Augustus - made travel and trade safer across the empire, connecting rural communities to wider markets and cultural currents. A farmer in Gaul or shepherd in Anatolia might never see Rome, but lived within a system Rome built and maintained.

Cultural Diversity: A World in One Empire

Rome's true genius lay not in its military or engineering - impressive as they were - but in the variety of human experience it encompassed.

By the Pax Romana's height, the Roman Empire included peoples speaking dozens of languages, worshipping hundreds of gods, eating different foods, wearing different clothes, and organizing family life according to diverse customs. Egyptians, Gauls, Greeks, Syrians, Berbers, Britons, and others lived under the same administration, paid the same taxes, and adhered to the same laws - while remaining distinct.

Rome's approach to diversity was pragmatic rather than ideological. The empire generally did not demand cultural conformity. Local languages continued; local religious practices persisted alongside the state religion; regional elites were often incorporated into administration, gaining citizenship and titles while maintaining identities. This flexibility was a strength, reducing conquest friction and easing governance.

Latin spread as the language of administration, law, and commerce - particularly in the west - while Greek remained dominant in eastern culture and trade. Merchants conducting business across the empire needed both. Soldiers stationed far from home encountered foreign gods, foods, and customs, often absorbing them. The Roman army was a remarkable engine of cultural mixing, drawing recruits from across the empire and stationing them far from origins.

This diversity, however, was not without tension. Conquered peoples bore wounds of defeat and the weight of imperial rule. Enslaved individuals, drawn from everywhere, represented the empire's darkest dimension of cultural mixing - stripped of identity and humanity. The cultural richness was real, but it rested on foundations of violence.

Yet, the cultural exchange experience produced something creative. New religious movements spread along trade routes. Artistic styles blended across regions. Foods, technologies, and ideas traveled throughout the empire. Rome absorbed as much as it imposed, resulting in a civilization of extraordinary complexity.

Quick Summary

- Augustus's creation of the Roman Empire in 27 BCE shaped daily life for millions across centuries.

- The Roman economy relied on both free and slave labor, with enslaved workers creating pressure on free working-class Romans.

- Urban life centered on public spaces - Forum, baths, markets - intertwining social, economic, and political life.

- Rural life, governed by agricultural rhythms, was harder and more isolated, though the Pax Romana improved connectivity and stability.

- The Pax Romana enabled economic development and cultural exchange previously impossible in the Mediterranean.

- Roman administration incorporated local elites and tolerated cultural differences, easing governance across vast territories.

- Cultural diversity within the empire was creative but coexisted with conquest violence and slavery's brutality.

The everyday life of the Roman Empire was neither the polished marble of its monuments nor the chaos of its crises. It was a vast, complicated, often contradictory civilization where millions pursued ordinary lives under extraordinary circumstances. Understanding this texture enables us to see Rome not as a distant myth, but as a real place filled with people whose world continues to shape ours.

PART 6
ART, CITIES, AND MATERIAL
POWER

Chapter 13

Persepolis

Somewhere in the highlands of what is now southern Iran, workers once carved the faces of twenty-three nations into stone - not as conquered peoples, but as bearers of gifts, walking in orderly procession toward a king who sat at the center of the known world. This image, etched repeatedly across the walls of Persepolis, encapsulates its core message.

Persepolis was not a city in the ordinary sense. It lacked bustling markets, dense residential quarters, and commercial importance. Instead, it embodied a vision. When Darius I began construction at Parsa around 518 BCE, he wasn't merely building a palace. He was crafting a monumental declaration that the Achaemenid Empire was the rightful hub of civilization, with its king ruling a divinely ordered world.

For nearly two centuries, Persepolis served as the ceremonial heart of that empire until Alexander the Great arrived in 330 BCE, answering the city's assertions with fire.

This chapter explores Persepolis's essence, significance, and construction - from the ideological ambitions to the monumental logistics required to raise it from a rocky plateau.

A Capital Built for Ceremony

Darius I chose a site set against a mountain backdrop in what is now Iran's Fars region, elevated and naturally defensible. This intentional design ensured security for the empire's treasures, archives, and symbolic authority.

Construction began around 518 BCE and continued under Darius's successors, including Xerxes I and Artaxerxes I. The project's multigenerational scope reflects its ambition. Darius's successors inherited and expanded his vision, each adding structures to the evolving complex.

Persepolis's functions were administrative, cultural, and ceremonial. As an administrative center, it housed the empire's records and tributes. Culturally, it drew craftsmen from Babylon, Egypt, Lydia, and Iran, fusing traditions into a distinctively Persian form. Ceremonially, it hosted the Nowruz celebrations, welcoming delegations bearing gifts for the king.

Architecture here was designed to be experienced in a procession. Visitors ascended a grand double staircase to the terrace, passed through the Gate of All Nations - flanked by colossal winged bulls - and moved through awe-inspiring spaces. Every step was choreographed, every surface a message.

The Apadana: A Room Built for Submission

The Apadana, the grand audience hall, was the terrace's most imposing structure, initially commissioned by Darius and completed under Xerxes. Its roof rested on 72 towering columns, an engineering marvel of its time. Only 13 remain, yet even these remnants convey the scale of what once was.

The Apadana wasn't meant for comfort but for the performance of imperial hierarchy. Standing in that hall among imposing columns and stone processions made one's place in the Achaemenid order unmistakable.

Stone as Ideology: The Reliefs of Persepolis

Persepolis Relief Scene

While its architecture communicated power through scale, Persepolis's reliefs conveyed it through narrative. Carved across staircases, doorways, and palace walls, these images form one of antiquity's most coherent political imagery programs.

The Apadana reliefs depict delegations from across the empire - Medes, Elamites, Babylonians, Egyptians, and more - each uniquely rendered in clothing, hairstyles, and gifts, walking peacefully toward the king. These images eschew violence, suggesting harmony and ordered authority under Achaemenid rule.

This sophisticated propaganda presents subjects as dignified participants, not subordinates. It argues that Persian rule was not oppression but order, portraying the king as the unifying force of the world.

The King and the Divine

Other reliefs highlight the sacred dimension of royal power, often depicting Darius and Xerxes beneath Ahura Mazda's winged symbol. The king isn't a god but an instrument of divine will, with authority from a cosmic source beyond human challenge.

This theological framing wasn't incidental. The Achaemenid Empire's diverse population - Persians, Babylonians, Egyptians, Greeks, and more - required an ideology that could accommodate everyone. By positing the king as an agent of universal divine order, the court crafted a unifying doctrine.

The reliefs were more than decoration; they were doctrine.

Craftsmanship Across Cultures

The reliefs' composite nature is noteworthy. Persian art of this period melded Mesopotamian, Egyptian, and Greek traditions, creating something distinctively Persian. The guardian figures at the Gate of All Nations echo Assyrian sculpture, while the processional friezes recall Egyptian temple reliefs. This visual language demonstrated the empire's cultural synthesis and elevation.

Persepolis didn't just conquer other civilizations - it absorbed and elevated them, and its art visibly proclaimed this claim.

Building the Mountain: Workforce and Logistics

Persepolis required more than vision; it demanded enormous, organized labor over decades on a remote plateau.

While ancient projects of this scale are often seen through coercion, Persepolis's records complicate this view. Elamite administrative tablets document payments in grain, wine, beer, and livestock to skilled craftsmen and laborers, suggesting some level of compensation.

The workforce's diversity mirrored the reliefs—an intentional reflection of imperial reach. Workers from across the empire, including Babylonians, Egyptians, Lydians, and Ionians, labored together. Darius acknowledged this multinational workforce as evidence of imperial power.

Stone, Timber, and Distance

Construction logistics were formidable. Stone was quarried locally, while cedar timber came from Lebanon, traveling great distances. Precious materials were drawn from far-flung imperial networks - the serene reliefs mirrored this imperial connectivity.

Coordinating materials and labor required a bureaucratic system as sophisticated as the architecture. The Elamite tablets reveal this administrative infrastructure, managing resources and workers across vast distances. Persepolis was not just a monument but a demonstration of Achaemenid power in practice.

The Fire of 330 BCE

For two centuries, Persepolis stood as the ceremonial heart, until Alexander the Great's arrival.

Captured in 330 BCE, Persepolis faced destruction. Whether the royal palace was burned by Alexander's deliberate order or an unruly celebration remains debated, as ancient sources provide conflicting accounts. Nonetheless, the result was clear. The palace burned, the archives were lost, and Persepolis's role as an imperial center vanished overnight.

Rediscovered by European travelers in the seventeenth century, Persepolis was designated a UNESCO World Heritage Site in 1979, affirming its historical significance.

Key Takeaways

- Founded by Darius I around 518 BCE, Persepolis served as the Achaemenid Empire's ceremonial capital.

- Its architecture was a choreographed expression of imperial power, centered on the Apadana audience hall.

- Reliefs depicted orderly delegations, presenting Achaemenid rule as harmonious and inclusive.

- Royal ideology linked the king to divine authority, accommodating the empire's diverse peoples.

- The art at Persepolis synthesized Babylonian, Egyptian, and Greek traditions into a unique Persian form.

- Administrative tablets reveal a multinational workforce, partially compensated for their labor.

- Alexander the Great's capture and destruction of Persepolis in 330 BCE ended its imperial prominence.

- Persepolis's ruins, a UNESCO World Heritage Site since 1979, remain a testament to its historical importance.

Persepolis leaves a lasting question: what does it mean to build something meant to endure forever, only to see it destroyed in a single night? The Achaemenid kings carved their vision of world order into stone, confident in its permanence. Yet, Alexander's fire posed a brutal counterargument. Paradoxically, the ruins of Persepolis have outlasted the empire that destroyed it, with its reliefs still resonating across 2,500 years.

Chapter 14
Imperial Cities

A city can be many things at once - throne room, treasury, symbol, and stage. The rulers of the Achaemenid Empire understood this better than most in the ancient world. Rather than anchoring their power to a single capital, they crafted a network of great cities, each serving a unique purpose in the governance of the largest empire the world had yet seen.

For the Achaemenids, governing from one place would have been political blindness. Their empire spanned from the Aegean coast to the fringes of the Indian subcontinent, encompassing diverse peoples, languages, and traditions. No single city could hold all that together. Persian kings moved strategically between capitals, each one addressing different audiences and functions. By understanding these cities, we gain insight into how the empire truly operated.

Pasargadae: Where It All Began

Cyrus the Great did not inherit an empire; he built one through military prowess, political acumen, and a remarkable instinct for treating conquered peoples. When he needed a capital worthy of his creation, he chose a site in Persia's heartland - now Fars province, Iran - and named it Pasargadae.

As the first dynastic capital of the Achaemenid Empire, Pasargadae bore Cyrus's unmistakable stamp. Unlike the dense, fortified urban centers common in the ancient Near East, Pasargadae was designed as an open, parklike complex. Its structures - palaces, audience halls, gardens - were spread across the landscape, projecting confidence.

At its core stood the tomb of Cyrus, a simple yet imposing limestone structure on a stepped platform. Ancient sources note that Alexander the Great visited the tomb and was moved by its inscription - though its exact wording remains debated. Nonetheless, the tomb became a revered site, anchoring the dynasty's myth.

Pasargadae also introduced the paradeisos, or royal garden - a defining feature of Achaemenid royal architecture. These irrigated parks were not just decorative; they demonstrated royal power over nature, proving the king could make the land flourish at will.

Despite its symbolic weight, Pasargadae had practical limitations. Located in a remote highland region, it was distant from the empire's most populous and economically vital areas. As the empire grew and administrative demands increased, the center of gravity began to shift.

Susa: The Empire's Administrative Heart

Susa had a long, layered history before the Achaemenids arrived. Originally the capital of the Elamite Empire, it was absorbed by Cyrus not as a ruined conquest but as a thriving city with deep institutional roots.

Cambyses II, Cyrus's successor, decisively shifted the royal seat to Susa. The move was practical: Susa's location at major trade and communication crossroads made it ideal for managing the empire. Its infrastructure provided a ready-made foundation for new rulers.

Under Darius I, Susa reached its zenith. He rebuilt and expanded the city with a vast palace complex using craftsmen and materials from across the empire. Inscriptions from the era meticulously note these sources: cedar from Lebanon, gold from Sardis and Bactria, ivory from Ethiopia and India. Susa's palace was a tangible inventory of the empire's reach.

As the nerve center of Achaemenid governance, Susa facilitated royal correspondence, received tributes, and was the reporting hub for satraps—the regional governors. Herodotus described the Persian royal road, a highway linking the western empire to its core, with Susa at its eastern end. Everything led to Susa.

The Logic of Many Capitals

Pasargadae and Susa were not the only significant cities. Darius I added Persepolis, a grand ceremonial capital, while Ecbatana served as a summer royal residence in the cooler highlands. This four-capital system was a deliberate policy, not indecision.

The multi-capital system reflected the Achaemenids' understanding of power. An empire of such magnitude couldn't be managed from one location. However, the king's movement between capitals conveyed strategic messages: in Babylon, he was the king of Babylon; in Susa, the heir to Elamite tradition; in Persepolis, the "king of kings" during the Nowruz festival, receiving tribute from across the known world.

Each capital fulfilled distinct roles. Persepolis handled ceremonial affairs - its reliefs depicted delegations from around the globe bringing gifts, symbolizing universal dominion. Susa managed bureaucracy. Ecbatana provided a summer retreat and proximity to northern frontiers. Babylon linked the kings to ancient urban traditions.

This flexibility granted the Achaemenid system resilience that centralized empires lacked. No single city's fall could collapse the entire structure. When Alexander the Great captured and burned Persepolis in 330 BC, the symbolic blow was great, but the administrative network, dispersed across multiple centers, allowed resistance to continue for years.

Legacy & Long-Term Impact

The Achaemenid multi-capital model left an enduring legacy. Later Persian dynasties, like the Parthians and Sasanians, adopted similar systems, ruling from multiple centers rather than a single seat. The idea that a vast empire required diverse capitals persisted.

Susa remained significant long after the Achaemenids fell, its layers of occupation - Elamite, Achaemenid, Hellenistic, Parthian - making it archaeologically rich. Pasargadae, however, quickly faded as the center of power moved, preserved mainly by its remoteness and the reverence for Cyrus's tomb.

Quick Summary

- Pasargadae, founded by Cyrus the Great, was the initial dynastic capital with an open design, notable for Cyrus's tomb.

- Susa, with deep Elamite roots, became the primary administrative center under Cambyses II and was expanded by Darius I.

- Darius I enhanced Susa into the empire's bureaucratic hub, bringing in materials and craftsmen from across the realm.

- Persepolis served as a ceremonial capital; Ecbatana was a seasonal royal residence, forming a four-city governance system.

- The multi-capital strategy allowed Persian kings to project authority across diverse regions and cultures.

- Each capital spoke to a different audience: Babylon connected the king to Mesopotamian tradition, Susa to Elamite heritage, Persepolis to Persian identity.

- The system's distributed nature provided resilience - no single city's fall could bring down the entire administrative apparatus.

What the Achaemenid kings built was more than architecture. It was a statement - about power, legitimacy, and the ability to hold together a vast world. This perspective resonated through centuries of Persian history, influencing later empires' approaches to the relationship between a ruler, a capital, and their territories.

Chapter 15
Art and Imperial Identity

When Augustus wanted the Roman world to understand what his reign meant, he didn't write a manifesto. He built one.

Across Rome and the wider empire, stone, marble, and bronze became the languages of political authority. Monuments rose not merely to commemorate victories but to define power itself - who held it, why they deserved it, and what it promised for the future. Under Augustus, art ceased to be mere decoration; it became a compelling argument.

Symbols Cut in Stone

Few objects capture this transformation more vividly than the Ara Pacis Augustae - the Altar of Augustan Peace. Commissioned in 13 BCE to celebrate Augustus' return from military campaigns in Gaul and Spain, it was a religious monument dedicated to Pax, the goddess of peace. Yet, every carved surface told a deeper story.

The altar's marble reliefs depicted a procession of the imperial family alongside priests, senators, and attendants - a carefully arranged portrait of Roman society moving in dignified order. Augustus himself is present, not as a distant deity, but as the first citizen, integrated within the community he claimed to serve. The message was deliberate and precise: not the chaos of the late Republic with its civil wars and assassinations, but Rome restored.

What made the Ara Pacis an effective political tool was its blend of sacred and civic imagery. Religious elements lent divine authority, while the procession scenes grounded that authority in human reality. Together, they argued that Augustus' peace was not just politically beneficial - it was cosmically ordained.

The Forum as Imperial Statement

The Ara Pacis was not alone. Around the same period, Augustus established the Forum of Augustus, a monumental public space that expanded the political vocabulary of marble and myth into Rome's civic life.

At its center stood a temple to Mars Ultor - Mars the Avenger - fulfilling a vow Augustus made before the Battle of Philippi in 42 BCE, where he and Mark Antony defeated Julius Caesar's assassins. This temple connected Augustus directly to Rome's martial heritage and to Julius Caesar, reinforcing the dynastic legitimacy he carefully constructed.

Lining the forum's colonnades were statues of Rome's great generals and heroes, stretching back to the city's mythological founders. Augustus placed himself at the culmination of this lineage - not as a revolutionary who overturned the Republic but as a natural heir to centuries of Roman greatness. In the Forum of Augustus, history seemed to lead to one man.

Cultural Blending and the Imperial Aesthetic

Augustus did not invent Roman art from nothing. He inherited a visual culture deeply shaped by Greek influence - and he used it with extraordinary sophistication.

Roman artists and architects had long admired and absorbed Greek forms: the Corinthian column, the idealized human figure, the narrative relief. Under Augustus, these influences crystallized into a distinctly Roman imperial aesthetic. Greek refinement was married to Roman civic purpose, resulting in art that felt timeless and authoritative, rooted in a classical tradition implying permanence and civilization.

This cultural blending served a political function. By channeling Greek artistic traditions - esteemed throughout the Mediterranean as the pinnacle of cultural achievement - Augustan art claimed that Rome was not just a military power but a civilizing force. The empire's reach was justified not just by its legions, but by its culture.

Simultaneously, Augustan monuments celebrated distinctly Roman values: pietas (duty to gods, family, and state), virtus (courage and excellence), and concordia (harmony). These were carved into altars, inscribed on temples, and woven into the visual fabric of public spaces. Every Roman who walked through the Forum of Augustus or witnessed a ceremony at the Ara Pacis absorbed these messages - whether they consciously registered them or not.

Art as the Architecture of Consent

What distinguished Augustan art from simple propaganda was its subtlety. Augustus understood that stark displays of power could breed resentment. Instead, his monuments invited Romans to see themselves as part of a shared project - the restoration of peace, order, and Roman greatness.

The Ara Pacis, for instance, depicted not just the imperial family but a wide cross-section of Roman society. Senators, priests, women, and children all appeared in the procession, each in their proper place.

This portrayed Roman society as harmonious and complete, with Augustus at its center but not towering above it. He was the first among equals - a carefully maintained and visually compelling fiction.

This approach helped smooth the profound political rupture that the transition from Republic to Empire represented. Romans who might have resisted the idea of a "king" could accept an emperor who presented himself through art as a restorer of tradition rather than its destroyer.

Key Takeaways

- The Ara Pacis Augustae, commissioned in 13 BCE, celebrated the peace Augustus brought after military campaigns abroad.

- Augustus used art and architecture systematically to legitimize his rule and communicate political messages to Roman society.

- The Forum of Augustus linked the emperor to Rome's heroic past, presenting him as the culmination of centuries of Roman greatness.

- Augustan art blended Greek aesthetic traditions with Roman civic values, projecting cultural authority alongside military power.

- Monuments like the Ara Pacis depicted Roman society as harmonious and ordered, with Augustus as its natural center.

- Art served as a tool of political transition, helping Romans accept imperial rule by framing it as the restoration of tradition.

- The legacy of Augustan visual culture shaped how subsequent emperors presented their own authority for centuries.

What Augustus built in marble outlasted everything he built in law. Empires can be dismantled; stone endures. The visual language he created - of peace, order, divine favor, and dynastic continuity - became the template for Roman emperors seeking to carve their own legitimacy into the city's enduring stones.

PART 7
MILITARY AND FRONTIERS

Chapter 16
The Persian Military System

A single army crossing a river on a bridge of boats is a logistical masterpiece. Xerxes I achieved this with such a vast army that, according to Herodotus, it took seven days and nights of continuous marching to cross the Hellespont.

While Herodotus's accounts may embellish details, they highlight the reality of the Persian military machine: vast, organized, and unparalleled in the ancient world. The Achaemenid Empire, founded by Cyrus the Great in 550 BCE, not only conquered territories but built a system for maintaining, traversing, and projecting power. Central to this system was an army that drew soldiers, resources, and tactics from diverse peoples across three continents.

To understand this army, it's essential to look beyond Greek portrayals of disorder and focus on the structure, logistics, and human diversity that made Persian military strength enduring and formidable.

The Architecture of an Empire's Army

Every military reflects its civilization, and the Persian army was no exception. Rooted in the traditions of the Medes, whom Cyrus the Great absorbed when founding the Achaemenid Empire, the Persians developed a hierarchical force capable of operating on an imperial scale.

At the heart of this structure was a decimal organization system. Units were formed in tens, hundreds, thousands, and ten thousands. The largest unit, the division of ten thousand, was known as the *Immortals*. This elite force served as the king's guard and the empire's reliable heavy infantry. Their name stemmed from the practice of replacing any fallen member immediately, maintaining the unit's constant strength.

Beneath the elite corps, the army consisted of infantry, cavalry, and specialist units. Infantry, including spearmen and archers, was crucial for Persian campaigns, with archers playing a pivotal role. Persian tactics often began with archery to weaken enemies before engaging in melee. This strategy, influenced by earlier Assyrian military practices, demonstrated tactical sophistication.

Cavalry added speed and power, enabling maneuvers like screening advances and pursuing enemies, capabilities unattainable by infantry alone.

Command, Hierarchy, and the King's Authority

Persian command flowed from the king. During major campaigns, the monarch often led personally, as with Darius I against the Scythians and Xerxes I in Greece in 480 BCE. This presence wasn't just symbolic; it centralized authority, enhanced legitimacy, and motivated troops more effectively than a distant commander.

Senior officers were primarily of Persian nobility or ruling classes of conquered peoples. Satraps, governors of the empire's provinces, had dual roles, managing both military and administrative duties. They raised and supplied regional contingents, making the satrapal system integral to administrative and military success.

Practically, this meant the Persian army was a coalition, drawing on diverse parts of the empire and commanded through a blend of royal and regional power. This structure offered extensive reach but introduced coordination challenges that could become vulnerabilities under pressure.

Moving an Empire: Logistics and Scale

An army of Persia's magnitude couldn't survive by foraging alone. Sustaining vast troops across Achaemenid campaign distances required sophisticated logistics.

Pontoon bridges were prime examples of Persian engineering. When Darius I and later Xerxes I crossed into Europe, these were meticulously planned and constructed. The Hellespont crossing involved numerous boats, cables, and a constructed surface for crossing. When a storm destroyed the first bridge, Xerxes ordered its reconstruction.

Persian logistics included supply lines and pre-positioned depots, with subject nations contributing according to proximity and importance to the empire. This tribute-and-supply system efficiently distributed burdens while ensuring army readiness.

Persia's logistical capacity was a form of power, enabling sustained campaigns over thousands of miles, influencing regional politics simply by existing.

Soldiers from Every Corner of the World

The Persian military's ethnic and cultural diversity set it apart. Cyrus the Great's policy of integrating conquered peoples extended to the military. Soldiers from across the empire served under Persian command, bringing unique weapons, styles, and traditions.

Herodotus documented Xerxes's diverse contingents into Greece - Medes, Persians, Lydians, Egyptians, Ethiopians, Indians, Bactrians, Scythians, and more. Each group retained distinct armor, weapons, and tactics.

This diversity was a strength, enabling the army to field a range of military capabilities from heavy infantry to siege engineers. Coordinating such a varied force demanded administrative skill and cultural flexibility, showcasing the Achaemenid system's organizational prowess.

The army mirrored the empire's approach: loyalty, tribute, and military service in exchange for cultural autonomy. It was a microcosm of Persia's successful governance approach.

Legacy and Long-Term Impact

The Achaemenid military system didn't end with the empire's decline. Later dynasties like the Parthians and Sassanians adapted its core, evolving towards systems historians compare to feudal models, where military service tied to land and noble status. This shift reflected political changes but built on Achaemenid foundations.

The Persian military demonstrated that military power relied on organization, logistics, and integrating diverse peoples into a cohesive force. Greek portrayals of the Persian army as disorganized did more to serve Greek interests than capture reality. The army that forged and maintained the largest empire of its time was far more sophisticated than mere numbers.

Quick Summary

- The Achaemenid Empire, founded by Cyrus the Great in 550 BCE, built a military capable of projecting power across continents.

- The Persian army used a decimal structure, with elite Immortals as its most renowned unit.

- Tactics involved combined forces, drawing from Assyrian influences.

- The king led major campaigns; regional satraps held military and administrative roles.

- Logistics included innovative engineering and a tribute system to maintain army readiness.

- The army's diversity included soldiers from across the empire, each contributing unique skills.

- Successors like the Parthians and Sassanians adapted this military tradition until the Arab conquests of 651 CE ended the Sassanian era.

The Persians created not just an army but a system that turned imperial diversity into a military asset, influencing future multi-ethnic military forces. The subsequent chapters will explore how this system met its challenges and revealed insights into ancient power dynamics.

Chapter 17
Persia and Greece in Context

Greco-Persian Conflict Map

The conflict between Persia and Greece is often introduced to students through the dramatic tale of the Battle of Thermopylae. However, this is just a glimpse of the complex interactions between these two ancient civilizations. To fully appreciate their historical relationship, it's essential to go beyond familiar narratives and explore the broader context, including the biases that have shaped our understanding.

Reframing the Greek Wars

The Greek-Persian wars, often depicted as a dramatic clash between East and West, have become legendary. These conflicts were more than just battles; they were moments of cultural and political significance. The Greeks saw themselves defending their way of life. Yet, for Persia, these were merely frontier skirmishes within a vast empire.

Understanding this difference in perspective is crucial. Persia was a sprawling empire with efficient administration, compared to the smaller, autonomous city-states of Greece. This asymmetry in power dynamics influenced the course of the wars. The famed Battle of Marathon and the naval engagement at Salamis were turning points that have been interpreted through a distinctly Greek lens. The Greeks celebrated these as heroic moments, while for the Persians, they were setbacks in an otherwise expansive rule.

Bias in Greek Sources

The primary records of these events come predominantly from Greek historians such as Herodotus. This has created a source bias, framing the Greeks as defenders of freedom against an eastern despot. Herodotus himself, known as the "Father of History," wrote compelling narratives but with a clear Greek bias.

Historians now recognize the need to contextualize these accounts. Persian sources, though less emphasized in historical education, reveal a more complex relationship. For Persia, the Greek conflicts were not existential threats but rather campaigns on the fringe of their empire. Persian reactions, diplomatic efforts, and cultural exchanges offer a richer understanding of this period.

The Interplay of Cultures

Beyond the battles, the interaction between Persia and Greece sparked significant cultural exchanges. Persian influence can be seen in Greek art, architecture, and even governance. Similarly, Greek ideas permeated the Persian world, exemplified by the adoption of some Greek practices by Persian elites.

The eventual conquests of Alexander the Great further entwined these cultures. His campaigns spread Hellenistic culture across the former Persian territories, blending with the existing traditions to create a vibrant, hybrid civilization.

Conclusion

The relationship between Persia and Greece was far more intricate than the simplistic narratives of textbooks suggest. Recognizing the biases in source material and appreciating the multidimensional interactions between these civilizations provide a more nuanced understanding. This broader perspective allows us to see past the mythologized accounts and appreciate the true nature of their historical encounters.

PART 8
SOURCES, CRISIS, AND FALL

Chapter 18
How We Know Persia

Every empire leaves behind both the legacies it intended to preserve and those it never meant to share. Persia left behind both.

When considering ancient Persia, many think of Greek writers: Herodotus with his sprawling *Histories*, Xenophon marching through hostile lands, and Aeschylus depicting Persian grief on the Athenian stage. These sources are invaluable but offer only part of the story - and a slanted one at that. The full picture of the Achaemenid Empire, founded by Cyrus the Great around 550 BCE and lasting until Alexander's conquest in 330 BCE, is drawn from a diverse and intricate archive: clay tablets buried under Persepolis, Aramaic administrative documents spread across the ancient Near East, Babylonian astronomical diaries, and royal inscriptions carved into unreachable cliff faces.

Each of these sources has distinct character, blind spots, and strengths. Together, they allow historians to reconstruct one of the greatest empires of the ancient world - imperfectly, and not without debate, but with a surprising depth and texture.

The Greek Lens: Vivid, Valuable, and Partial

Greek accounts of Achaemenid Persia are both vivid and problematic.

Herodotus, writing in the fifth century BCE, invested significant effort into describing the Persian Wars, Persian customs, and its kings' characters. His *Histories* remain indispensable, offering unique insights into Persian administration, religious practices, and military organization.

However, Herodotus, a Greek writing for Greeks after a victorious war, often portrayed Persians as decadent and tyrannical, serving the Greek narrative of superiority. Xenophon, offering a soldier's perspective in his *Anabasis*, captured the Persian landscape and provincial power structures but similarly aimed to reflect well on Greek prowess.

Aeschylus's tragedy, *The Persians*, is the oldest surviving Greek drama but doesn't serve as a Persian source. Instead, it reflects Athenian imaginings of a defeated enemy and provides minimal reliable insight into Persian experiences.

In short, Greek sources are crucial yet insufficient. They provide narrative energy but view Persia through an Athenian lens.

Babylonian and Aramaic Records: The Empire's Own

Paperwork

More revealing than Greek narratives are the administrative records in the Achaemenid Empire's languages.

Babylonia, a literate culture millennia before Cyrus's conquest in 539 BCE, continued producing records under Persian rule. Babylonian cuneiform tablets recorded business transactions, temple accounts, and astronomical diaries, juxtaposing celestial events with significant political milestones. These diaries provide precise chronological markers that assist in dating events across the ancient world.

Aramaic became the empire's administrative lingua franca, essential for governing diverse peoples. Aramaic documents, found from Egypt to Central Asia, illustrate the empire's vast bureaucratic reach.

These records may lack heroic tales, but they reveal the empire's operational mechanics - grain allocations, legal disputes, tax records - highlighting an empire that held together across extensive territories.

The Persepolis Tablets: Voices from the Archive

The discovery of tens of thousands of clay tablets at Persepolis in the 1930s dramatically transformed our understanding of the Achaemenid Empire.

Persepolis, a ceremonial heart and administrative hub, housed tablets that survived a fire set by Alexander in 330 BCE. These tablets contain no royal propaganda but administrative records: rations for workers, payments, and travel authorizations. Written in Elamite, they cover roughly 509 to 458 BCE. Known as the Persepolis Fortification Archive and Treasury Tablets, they offer unparalleled insights into the empire's workings.

They reveal an empire managed with logistics, fairness, and detailed record-keeping, countering the Greek portrayal of despotic rule. While not benevolent by modern standards, the reality was more nuanced than any single tradition suggests.

Reading the Empire Whole

Combining these source traditions offers a richer understanding than any one alone could provide.

Greek sources deliver narrative and drama - wars, personalities, and crises that shaped perceptions of Persia. Babylonian and Aramaic records offer chronology and administrative reality.

The Persepolis tablets provide a rare glimpse from within, depicting the ordinary business of an extraordinary empire.

No source is neutral. Greek writers sought to explain a war, Babylonian scribes recorded transactions, and Persian administrators tracked resources. Historians must read each with awareness of its purpose and limitations.

Quick Summary

- The Achaemenid Empire, from 550 BCE to 330 BCE, is reconstructed from diverse source traditions.

- Greek writers like Herodotus and Xenophon provide narrative accounts but reflect Greek biases.

- Aeschylus's *The Persians* serves as cultural commentary, not documentary evidence.

- Babylonian cuneiform records, including astronomical diaries, offer chronological data and insights into Persian rule.

- Aramaic was the Achaemenid Empire's administrative language, revealing its bureaucratic reach.

- The Persepolis Fortification Archive and Treasury Tablets offer an inside view of administration from 509 to 458 BCE.

- Together, these sources depict a complex, multiethnic, systematically organized empire.

Understanding Persia means interpreting each source with an awareness of what it reveals and conceals. The Achaemenid world was vast, and thankfully, many voices have survived to tell its story.

Chapter 19
Decline of the Empire

Rome's fall was gradual, unraveling over centuries, crisis by crisis, until the once-formidable state could no longer sustain itself.

Few historical events have been examined as thoroughly as Rome's collapse. Scholars have long debated its causes, which appear multifaceted. Evidence shows the decline stemmed from a combination of political chaos, financial exhaustion, military overextension, and a governing structure that eventually collapsed under its own weight. Understanding Rome's unraveling offers insights into the fragility of complex civilizations.

This chapter examines three central forces that propelled Rome's collapse: the succession struggles that turned imperial power into a deadly contest, the overwhelming administrative burden of governing a vast empire, and the regional revolts indicating Rome's weakened grip on its territories.

The Bloodiest Game: Succession Struggles

Power in Rome was never easily transferred. Lacking a fixed succession rule, transitions became critical points of vulnerability. This flaw, manageable during stable times, became catastrophic during the Crisis of the Third Century (180-284 CE), often referred to as the "Terrible Third Century."

In this era, the imperial throne changed hands frequently through assassination, military coups, and civil wars. Rival generals declared themselves emperor, engaging their legions in conflict and leaving borders exposed. Soldiers, tasked with defending Rome's frontiers, instead fought each other for control of the empire.

These struggles were more than political inconvenience; they drained resources, disrupted trade, and undermined governmental legitimacy. An emperor who seized power violently had to consolidate it, buying loyalty, eliminating rivals, and rewarding the troops who helped him ascend. Consequently, empire governance became secondary.

The instability fostered short-term thinking at Rome's highest levels. Emperors, anticipating assassination, had little incentive for long-term reforms. Investing in infrastructure or diplomacy seemed futile given the imminent threat of coups. The crisis weakened individual emperors and the institution of the emperorship itself.

Julian the Apostate exemplifies the personal and ideological nature of these struggles. His attempt to reverse the Christianization of the empire and restore paganism was both political and religious, highlighting ongoing contests about Rome's identity as the empire's foundations weakened.

A Machine Too Large to Run: Administrative Strain

At its peak, Rome's territories stretched from Britain to Mesopotamia, posing immense logistical challenges. By the third and fourth centuries, the empire's administrative systems showed significant strain.

Economic pressures compounded these challenges. Inflation devalued currency, while heavy taxes burdened provincial agricultural communities, the backbone of Rome's economy. The reliance on slave labor, productive in earlier centuries, created structural rigidities hindering economic adaptation. As military conquests slowed, so did the influx of new slaves, one of Rome's primary economic engines.

Maintaining the military grew costlier as external threats multiplied. The fiscal discipline needed to sustain the legions was hard to achieve amid political chaos and economic contraction. Emperors debased currency to cover costs, spurring inflation, increased taxation, and provincial resentment.

This formed a vicious cycle. The empire needed revenue for security, insecurity disrupted economic activity, and revenue generation faltered. Administrative systems, designed for a stable, expanding empire, struggled with a contracting, fragmenting one.

The Edges Begin to Break: Regional Revolts

As central authority weakened, the periphery resisted. Regional revolts became common during the empire's decline, highlighting a deeper erosion of loyalty to Rome.

Provinces once integrated into the empire's economic and political life began feeling more cost than benefit from this relationship. Heavy taxation without effective protection, currency debasement, and civil war disruptions fed local grievances. With legions distracted by internal conflicts, provincial populations often had to fend for themselves, culminating in rebellion.

External military threats further destabilized frontier regions. The combination of external pressure and internal discontent made territories harder to retain. Once fragmentation began, it was challenging to reverse.

These revolts were rational responses to a central government that could no longer provide order, security, or prosperity.

Key Takeaways

- Rome's decline spanned centuries, driven by overlapping political, economic, and military pressures, rather than a singular event.

- The Crisis of the Third Century (180-284 CE) was a pivotal period with rapid imperial succession, civil wars, and institutional breakdown.

- Succession struggles created instability, undermining governance and draining military resources.

- Economic decline - marked by inflation, taxation, and currency debasement - weakened administrative and defensive capabilities.

- Administrative strain hindered effective governance of vast territories, especially as fiscal pressures increased.

- Regional revolts indicated the erosion of provincial loyalty and the empire's fading capacity to protect its territories.

- Julian the Apostate's efforts to restore paganism underscored the contested nature of Rome's identity even during its decline.

- These forces collectively led to the fragmentation and eventual fall of the Western Roman Empire.

Rome's decline underscores the limits of scale, costs of instability, and how powerful systems can be undone by pressures they generate. Its collapse reshaped Europe and the Mediterranean world, laying the groundwork for the medieval era that emerged from its ruins.

Chapter 20
Alexander and the End

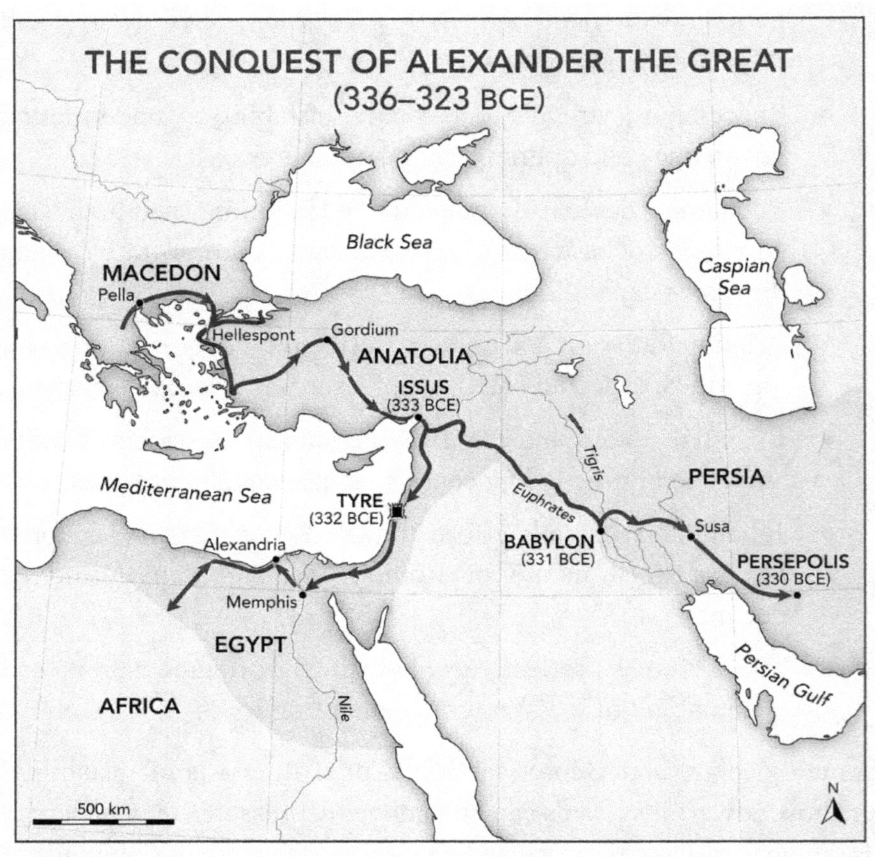

Alexander's Conquest

In thirteen years, Alexander of Macedon conquered more of the known world than any general before him. Yet, upon his death in Babylon at thirty-two, the empire he built began to fracture almost immediately. What he left behind proved more enduring than any borders on a map.

Few figures in history compressed such ambition, violence, and consequence into so short a life. Alexander's campaigns between 336 and 323 BCE reshaped three continents - not just politically, but culturally, linguistically, and intellectually. His armies carried Greek ideas from the Aegean to the edges of the Indian subcontinent, seeding concepts that outlasted each successor's kingdom. To understand the ancient world after him, one must grasp what Alexander set in motion and why it was so difficult to halt.

The March That Changed the World

Alexander became king of Macedon in 336 BCE following the assassination of his father, Philip II. At twenty, he solidified his grip on Greece and, within two years, crossed into Asia Minor. This campaign of conquest would not end until his death eleven years later.

His route was staggering in ambition. Advancing east and south, Alexander swept through Asia Minor, dismantling Persian resistance at the Granicus River and Issus. He claimed Egypt without significant opposition, as the Egyptians welcomed him more as a liberator than a conqueror. Moving deeper into the Persian heartland, he defeated Darius III decisively at Gaugamela in 331 BCE and then sacked Persepolis, the symbolic heart of the Achaemenid Empire.

Still, he pressed on.

By the time his exhausted army refused to march further east in 326 BCE - standing at the banks of the Hyphasis River in modern northwestern India - Alexander had amassed an empire stretching from Greece through Egypt, across Persia, and into Central Asia. No single ruler had ever controlled so much territory.

He founded cities along the way, planting outposts of Greek culture and administration. The most consequential was Alexandria in Egypt, established in 331 BCE. It became a center of scholarship, commerce, and cultural exchange that defined the Hellenistic age long after Alexander himself was gone.

Alexander died in Babylon in 323 BCE. The cause remains debated - fever, excessive drinking, poison, or some combination - but the result was clear. He left no clear successor, only an empire too large for any single heir to hold.

The Fracture and the Flowering

What followed Alexander's death was not simply collapse but transformation.

His generals - known as the Diadochi or "successors" - spent decades fighting over his inheritance. By the early third century BCE, the empire had fragmented into a cluster of competing kingdoms: the Ptolemaic kingdom in Egypt, the Seleucid empire across much of the former Persian territory, the Antigonid dynasty in Macedonia and Greece, and several smaller states.

These were not Greek kingdoms in the classical sense. They were hybrid states where Macedonian rulers governed largely non-Greek populations, and Greek culture mingled with Egyptian, Persian, Babylonian, and Indian traditions.

This fusion is what historians call the Hellenistic world, and in its way, it was more interesting than the conquests that created it.

Greek became the common language of commerce, diplomacy, and intellectual life across an enormous territory. A merchant in Alexandria, a philosopher in Antioch, and a bureaucrat in Babylon might all conduct their affairs in the same tongue. This linguistic unity - unprecedented in the ancient world - allowed ideas to travel with remarkable speed and range.

What Survived the Conqueror

The political structures Alexander built did not last. His empire divided within a generation, and the Hellenistic kingdoms eventually fell - most famously when Rome absorbed the last of them, Ptolemaic Egypt, in 30 BCE with Cleopatra VII's death. Yet, the cultural legacy proved far more resilient than any dynasty.

Greek art, architecture, and philosophy spread across three continents, blending with local traditions to produce something neither purely Greek nor purely local. Hellenistic sculpture became more expressive and emotionally charged than its classical predecessors. Hellenistic science - centered especially at Alexandria's famous Library and Museum - produced advances in mathematics, astronomy, and medicine that would not be surpassed for centuries.

Alexander's campaigns also introduced a politically charged idea: divine kingship. In Egypt, he was recognized as a pharaoh and son of the god Amun. His successors adopted similar claims, merging Greek political authority with the religious traditions of the peoples they ruled. This concept - that a king could be not merely a ruler but a living god - would ripple into Roman imperial ideology and beyond.

Perhaps most significantly, Greek became the language in which early Christianity spread. When the New Testament was written, it was in Greek - the common tongue of the Hellenistic world that Alexander had shaped. The reach of that single linguistic legacy is immense.

Key Takeaways

- Alexander reigned from 336 to 323 BCE, conquering territory from Greece to northwestern India.

- He founded numerous cities, most importantly Alexandria in Egypt, a major center of culture and learning.

- Alexander died in Babylon in 323 BCE at age thirty-two, leaving no clear successor.

- His generals, the Diadochi, divided his empire into competing Hellenistic kingdoms.

- Greek became the common language across the Hellenistic world, enabling the spread of ideas across three continents.

- Hellenistic culture blended Greek traditions with Egyptian, Persian, and other local influences in art, science, and religion.

- Alexander's campaigns introduced the concept of divine kingship, influencing later empires.

- The Hellenistic cultural legacy endured long after political structures collapsed, shaping Rome and early Christianity alike.

Alexander's empire barely lasted a generation in its original form, but the world he created - Greek-speaking, culturally hybrid, intellectually restless - endured for centuries. Rome would conquer the Hellenistic kingdoms one by one, yet Rome itself would be conquered by Greek culture, as the poet Horace observed. Alexander died young, but the world he set in motion continued long after his passing.

Chapter 21
Legacy of Persia

Empires rarely die cleanly. They dissolve slowly, leaving traces of their institutions, the practices of their administrators, and the memory of their grandeur - elements that the next civilization inherits, often without acknowledgement.

Few empires embody this truth more powerfully than Persia. Even after the Achaemenids faded from power and Alexander's conquest reshaped the world, the Persian idea endured. It resurfaced under the Parthians, crystallized again with the Sasanians, and influenced empires from Byzantium to the early Islamic caliphates. To understand how the ancient world transitioned into the medieval, we must explore what Persia left behind.

The Long Influence of Empire

The Parthians: Heirs by Geography, Heirs by Design

When the Arsacid dynasty established the Parthian Empire around 238 BCE, they inherited a landscape molded by centuries of Persian rule - roads, satrapies, trade networks, and the expectation that a great empire should function through layers of local authority rather than direct command.

The Parthians, ruling from roughly 238 BCE to 224 CE, embraced this legacy. Their famously decentralized empire functioned through a constellation of local rulers and nobles who retained autonomy in exchange for loyalty and tribute. This was a deliberate system, allowing the Parthians to govern vast territories without the burdensome bureaucracy of centralized states.

Militarily, the Parthians became legendary. Their cavalry - heavy cataphracts and agile horse archers capable of firing while retreating - defined Near Eastern military power for centuries. The Roman legions, accustomed to infantry warfare, struggled against Parthian tactics, as exemplified by their devastating defeat at the Battle of Carrhae in 53 BCE, where the general Crassus and tens of thousands of Romans fell to Parthian forces.

Despite their success, the Parthians remain elusive to historians. Modern political instability has hampered archaeological efforts, and much primary scholarship exists in Persian, limiting its integration into broader studies. What is known paints a picture of a sophisticated civilization blending Iranian, Hellenistic, and Mesopotamian cultures.

The Sasanians: Consolidation and Continuity

In 224 CE, Ardashir I overthrew the last Arsacid ruler, founding the Sasanian Empire - a dynasty lasting until the Arab conquests of 642 CE. This transition is often seen as a sharp break, but it was more gradual.

Material culture and records from the early Sasanian period reveal strong continuities with Parthian systems. Military strategies, bureaucratic practices, and aspects of royal ideology carried forward. The Sasanians did not erase the Parthian order; they reorganized it, centralizing power under a strong monarchy.

The Sasanians pursued greater ambition. They centralized the empire's structure with a formal court hierarchy and established Zoroastrianism as a state pillar, linking religion to monarchy - a practice that echoed through successive Persian and Islamic political cultures.

At its height, the Sasanian Empire spanned from Mesopotamia to Central Asia, maintaining a rivalry with the Roman and Byzantine empires. Their long conflicts sapped both empires, contributing to their vulnerability to the Arab expansion in the seventh century.

Culturally, the Sasanian era witnessed a flourishing of Persian literature, art, and architecture. The administrative language evolved, laying the groundwork for classical Persian, a linguistic heritage that enriched the Islamic world.

What One Empire Passes to the Next

The enduring legacy of both the Parthian and Sasanian empires was their institutions. The concept of a layered, multiethnic empire linked by shared ideology and a strong central authority passed from the Achaemenids to the Parthians, then to the Sasanians, and finally into the structures of early Islamic caliphates.

When Arabs conquered the Sasanian Empire, they preserved much of its bureaucracy, employing the same Persian administrators. The Persian concept of kingship, with its ceremonially elaborate court, profoundly influenced the governance of the Abbasid caliphate, blurring the lines between Sasanian and Islamic practices.

Why Persia Still Matters

Reframing the Story of the Ancient World

Western historical narratives often center on Greece and Rome, casting Persia primarily as an antagonist vanquished by Alexander and largely ignoring its broader significance.

This perspective obscures more than it clarifies.

Persia was not merely a backdrop to Greek achievements. It was a civilization of similar sophistication, greater territorial reach, and lasting administrative impact. The Achaemenid governance system - tolerant of local customs and organized through regional satrapies - was a significant model of large-scale human organization, influencing Parthians, Sasanians, and medieval Islam.

Recentering Persia in ancient history enhances, rather than diminishes, the achievements of Greece and Rome, offering a more accurate understanding of how power, culture, and knowledge moved throughout the ancient world.

Persian art, literature, and religious thought persisted despite changing political powers. Zoroastrian ideas of dualism and divine judgment left their mark on Judaism, Christianity, and Islam. The Persian *pairidaeza* (royal garden) inspired the word "paradise," a testament to Persia's pervasive yet often unrecognized influence.

Quick Summary

- The Parthian Empire (238 BCE-224 CE) utilized decentralized administration, building on earlier Persian models.

- Parthian cavalry innovations challenged Roman tactics and shaped regional warfare.

- The Sasanian Empire (224-642 CE) followed the Parthians through gradual change, maintaining administrative continuities.

- Sasanian rulers centralized power, linking it to Zoroastrian religious identity.

- Both empires transmitted Persian traditions into the early Islamic world post-Arab conquest.

- Persia's legacy is often undervalued in Western-centric historical narratives focused on Greece and Rome.

- Persian contributions influenced language, religion, governance, and art, impacting the medieval world significantly.

Persia's influence continued well beyond the torching of Persepolis in 330 BCE and the Arab conquests centuries later. It endured in the practices of administrators, the language of rulers, and the architecture of courts from Baghdad to Bukhara. Studying Persia reveals how some of history's most influential forces persist quietly, shaping the future long after their apparent end.

Congratulations on reaching the end of this book. By finishing it, you've taken a meaningful journey through one of the most remarkable empires in history - one that shaped governance, culture, and connections across continents in ways that still echo today. I hope this book has given you not only a clearer understanding of the Persian Empire, but also a new perspective on how complex, sophisticated, and influential it truly was.

If you found this book valuable, engaging, or thought-provoking, I would truly appreciate it if you could take a moment to leave a review. Even a short review makes a big difference - it helps other readers discover the book and supports the continued creation of high-quality historical content like this.

Thank you again for your time, your curiosity, and your interest in history.